The Father's Love

Volume 1:
What Seek Ye?

By Fount Shults

© 2020 by Fount Shults

The Father's Love: Volume One

The Father's Love was previously published in 2007 under the title *Father's Love Journey: A Devotional Commentary on the Gospel of John*.

This volume is part one of a three-volume set which was revised and updated in 2020.

All rights reserved. No part of this publication may be reproduced or transmitted in any form without prior written permission from the author. The only exception is brief quotations for reviews or manuscripts where source is credited.

All Scripture quotations are the author's own — which are influenced by the Revised Standard Version. Copyright © 1952, 1971 Zondervan Bible Publishers.

Fount Shults has been married to his wife, best friend, and partner in ministry, Lynda, since 1964. They have six children, 12 grandchildren and two great grandchildren. Together they founded *On Word Ministries* in 1987.

Fount is available for speaking engagements. For further information please visit www.onword.org or write to fount@onword.org

Published by Patrick Selvey
ISBN: 978-0-9992334-3-6

Dedicated to all my students

Table of Contents

Foreword by Bob Sorge 7

Preface 11

Introduction 15

Chapter One: The Significance of Signs 19

Chapter Two: The Goal of Believing 37

Chapter Three: The Significance of Signs 49

Chapter Four: Disciples and Presence 59

Chapter Five: Transition from the Old to the New 71

Chapter Six: The Bosom of the Father 87

Chapter Seven: What Do You Seek? 115

Chapter Eight: Three Classes of People 127

Foreword

If I told you I knew the Master Key to the Christian life, would I pique your interest? Would you like to know what it is? The truth is, there is one single key that, when engaged, opens to us the panoramic vistas of Kingdom possibilities. And I know what it is.

What's more, I'll tell you what it is—if you'll just hang with me for a few minutes. The answer is so important that is deserves a little bit of build-up. Allow me to set it up with a hypothetical situation.

They banish you to live by yourself on a remote Pacific island, and they tell you that can only take one book of the Bible with you. Question: Which book would you take?

If it were me, I'd be in a whole lot of pain. You're telling me that I've got to toss 65 of the 66 Bible books and narrow it down to just one? Ugh, this is awful! I can't think of one book I could possibly do without. Psalms? I live in that book every day, don't take Psalms away from me! And Hebrews, I couldn't survive without Hebrews. Nor Romans. Isaiah! Don't touch Isaiah! Revelation – just try and take Revelation away from me. Job? Job is my buddy. Deuteronomy? I'm in love with that book! Acts? How could any-

The Father's Love

body live without the book of Acts? And then there's Ephesians – ah, Ephesians!

You're serious? I have to choose only one Bible book to keep for the rest of my life? Whew, this is tough! But if you're really gonna force me – I mean, if I really had to choose just one book of the Bible – I think I'd have to... uh...mmm...uh...I'd have to go with John. Final answer. The Gospel of John.

Wow, what a book! It's just gotta be one of your favorite books in the whole Bible. John's account is an unparalleled beholding of Jesus that sets your heart to burning for a relationship with the Father. Oh, the wonder of the Man, Christ Jesus! Oh, the wonder of His Father's embrace.

Then if they said, "Narrow it down to one chapter," I'd *really* be in trouble! What? Throw away 20 chapters and keep only *one* of John's 21 chapters? Don't take chapter 14 away from me! Nor chapter 3. Nor 17. Don't remove the crucifixion and resurrection in chapters 19-20! I've got 20 reasons why I can't cut any of the chapters. I'm in pain over here. I've got to choose just one chapter in the Gospel of John?? Well, if you absolutely *made* me choose just one chapter, I think I'd choose...um...mmm...uh...I'd have to go with...chapter 15. You forced me into it. Give me John 15.

Why chapter 15?

Because it's got the key. The Master Key. When I say it, you're going to go, "That's so simple!" And you're right. The Master Key to the Christian life is a very simple invitation from Jesus' lips: "'Abide in My love'" (John 15:9). There, that's it.

Foreword

"Abide in My love." So simple—and yet the greatest challenge you'll ever face. It's what the human heart longs for—an intimate, knowing, reciprocating, fiery love relationship with He is "The Desire Of All Nations" (Hag. 2:7) It's here that we find our reason for being. Herein is true success. Nothing else exhilarates the human spirit like the wonder of beholding the extravagant beauty of the One who died for us.

"Abide in my love." You can explore that goldmine for the rest of your days and at the end of your life realize that you hardly scratched the surface of the glorious depths of the love of Christ.

Why am I talking like this? Because the book you hold in your hands has been crafted specially to guide your steps into an abiding love relationship with Jesus Christ as he abides in the Father and the Father abides in Him. A book could hold no nobler purpose. Fount Shults lays the gospel of John plainly before us as a roadmap to intimacy with the Father in Jesus Christ.

Fount has the expertise to write a book that would have impressed us with its footnotes and quotations from erudite sources. Instead, he chose to write from the heart, in order to engage our heart. Simply because he wants us to see Jesus and, in seeing Him, to see the Father.

If you come away saying, "Now I know the Book of John," you will have missed Fount's message. If you hear from the heart, you'll come away saying, "I'm seeing Jesus, and His Father, like never before."

Fount was my classroom teacher 40 years ago when I was a Bible School student. Even back then his teachings on the Gospel of John impacted my life. My point is that this book is like a flask of well-aged wind. Drink deeply of every chapter. May the intoxicating love of Christ capture your soul!

Bob Sorge

Conference Speaker

Author of 24 books including
Secrets of the Secret Place,
and Exploring Worship.

Preface

My life and ministry have been greatly influenced by the Bible. I make no apologies. Almost as soon as I learned to read, I was devouring and trying to live by the Proverbs. My childhood church was a fundamentalist, Bible-believing community. We were taught that the Bible contained the true doctrines and the true way to live. I got the impression that our group was the only ones who really understood the Bible. Everyone else was deceived or confused. One of our pet doctrines had to do with water baptism. Baptism in water was the event that brought you into the fold as a true member. I wanted that.

It was the Summer of 1945, in Carlsbad, New Mexico. I still remember the sermon the evangelist preached that night. It was from Hebrews 12:1. The preacher said we must run the race according to the rules to gain the crown of life. As an almost nine-year-old boy, I wanted to run that race, I wanted to win that crown, I wanted to hear those words, "Well done." So, I went down to the front and they baptized me that night. Something real happened in that water. When I came up the congregation was singing, "All to Jesus I surrender." And I knew I had surrendered all. That song is still with me.

I began to pay attention to every sermon and every Sunday school lesson. For me it was not about going to heaven when I die.

I wanted to run the race and win the crown. The biblical world was becoming my world long before I understood the concept of "world" as distinct from the earth full of people. I would later learn that different people groups had different worldviews, different ideas about how the system we call "the world" is structured. Without realizing it, my worldview was being formed by the religious community of my youth.

A worldview is a personal and communal idea about how things work, what we need to say or do to experience a good life here and now and (for the religious) to go to heaven when we die. Early in my life I discovered the Gospel of John. That book has informed my worldview and continues to shift my concept of the "world" to this day. It was written in simple language but there was a depth that spoke profoundly into my spirit long before I knew I had a spirit. As I look back on those early years, I realize how inadequate my view of the world was. But despite the religious biases of my childhood community, I was able to grow beyond them as I matured.

The Gospel of John was my favorite class in undergraduate school. I worked my way through college preaching in small country churches. Even then John's Gospel was among my favorite books to quote from. I learned Greek and read the Gospel in the original language. I earned a Master of Arts degree with Church History and Greek as a double major and later earned a PhD in the Hebrew language. After I graduated, I began to teach in various state colleges and later in Bible Colleges. I have taught through the Gospel more times than I can count and some portion of it has been a text for almost every sermon I preached. My point is this: John has been my constant companion for over 70 years.

Preface

This volume is the first of three projected volumes on John's Gospel. All three volumes will contain what I call devotional commentary. By that I mean it is not intended to be read as an academic, scholarly work. The intent is to open a way to experience the presence of the one about whom John wrote. It is never enough to learn doctrines and gather information on the life of one who lived *"once upon a time, in a land far away."* My desire is that my readers might have a personal encounter with the one to whom the "signs" in John are pointing.

The foundational thought of all three volumes is the concept that a sign is something that points beyond itself to something other than and quite different from the sign itself. There is no food value in a sign that points to a restaurant. In the same way, memorizing and quoting verses from the Bible has no spiritual food value without a personal relationship with the one about whom the Bible speaks. This concept threatens the fundamentalists I grew up with. They placed the Bible on a pedestal it was not designed to occupy. It was as though John 1:1 reads, "In the beginning was the Bible, and the Bible was with God, and the Bible was God."

John's use of signs was designed to dismantle a concept that placed the Torah (the Jewish Bible) over a relationship with God. This first volume is my attempt to make clear John's approach to storytelling, an approach which is different from the other Gospels. The study of the Hebrew language and culture enabled me to read this Gospel through the eyes of the Jewish culture of the first century. In this first volume you will find the stories in John interpreted as signs. The purpose is to illustrate the significance of the fact that

John was not trying to write a biography of the life of Jesus. He was using the Jewish *midrashic* method of storytelling.

John was a Jew who walked with Jesus and came to know him as the Son of God. After the destruction of Jerusalem in 70 A.D., the Jewish nation had ceased to exist. The identity of the people as a people was in danger of being lost as well. The Christian Jews became a threat to the Jewish community's identity because they were loosening their commitment to rigid interpretations of the Torah and embracing some of the Gentile attitudes toward food and purity laws. The Jewish leaders of John's latter days began to cast those who believed in Jesus out of their synagogues to avoid being corrupted by their presence.

That was about sixty years after the death of Jesus. John's writing was designed to encourage his fellow believers to maintain their confidence in face of the persecution they were experiencing from their synagogue leaders. He probably had the Gentile believers in his mind as well since they were also being persecuted. John used the term "Jew" to refer to the religious leaders who rejected Jesus as the Jewish Messiah. That which appears to be *antisemitic* in John is only *"anti-control-freak"* leadership. There are many Gentile leaders in that category and John's anathema applies to them as well.

My hope is that, as you read this first volume you will experience enough personal awakening to anticipate the next two volumes as they become available.

The invitation of these volumes is, *"Come and see, look upon the one whom we have pierced"* (John 19:37). Have a nice journey into the mystery of the Father, who was and is in Jesus the Christ reconciling the world to himself by the Spirit (II Cor. 5:19).

Introduction

Most of the material in this series was originally published as one volume called *Father's Love Journey*. That book never appeared in bookstores because I only made copies available to individuals in the churches where I preached while I was itinerating. Several churches used that book as a text for their adult Sunday School classes and a few home prayer groups also used it. I took it out of print when I retired from being an itinerating professor. At the encouragement of a former student, Patrick Selvey, I am now making it available as an e-book in three volumes. It will also be available in paperback for those who prefer paper.

This introduction will be short because the first chapters of this volume are an introduction to the method John used to present the good news of Jesus the Christ to the Jewish community and to Gentile Christians of his day. These volumes will be an exposition of John's perspective of what happened to *this man Jesus* to show why his Gospel is so different from the Synoptic Gospels, Matthew, Mark, and Luke.

Throughout all three volumes there is a "play" with two phrases: *This man* and *Thatman*. *Thatman* echoes the wealthy superhero who fought crime by swooping down from above and bringing justice. By that figure I point to the many who saw Jesus as the Messiah they were expecting rather than seeing him as the one he was. By the figure *"this man"* I present Jesus as the one John the Baptist pointed to when he said, "Behold the Lamb of God." I borrowed that term from the question the gatekeeper asked Peter at the trial of Jesus: "Are you *this man's* disciple?" He was not an imaginary figure; he was a specific individual who lived at a specific time in a specific geographical location.

John's focus was on the contrast between those who are blind and those who see. Jesus can be viewed from the perspective of what the natural eye can see, or the natural mind can perceive. That is a way of seeing which is blind to what Paul called the unseen realm. Jesus can also be viewed through the eyes of one who has "washed in the Pool of Siloam" and received spiritual insight (John 9).

My goal in this first volume is fourfold: First, to draw the reader into a deeper personal experience of the real presence of Jesus among us today. No matter how deep you have gone, a deeper level is available. Second, to expose some of the structures of John's Gospel and show how those structures help us discover deeper meanings in the text. Third, to show the significance of the concept of sign in John's presentation of the life of Jesus. And fourth, to demonstrate the unity of John's Gospel with Paul's writing and with the whole of the Bible.

The structures in John's Gospel are the hermeneutical keys to the meaning of the text. The structures are well known among those who study the Hebrew poetry of the Old Testament. Hebrews are different from Greeks. To the Greeks, the noun is primary. The form of a *thing* as it appears to the eye determines its value. To the Hebrews, the verb is primary. The form of a *story* as it sounds to the ear determines its value. The goal of the stories is to create pictures of reality in the imagination. So, the Greeks produced material works of art (including theater) to be viewed by the community, while the Hebrews produced stories to be told around the family circle and in their synagogues. That difference is what distinguishes Jewish literature from Greek literature.

In this volume we will be dealing with the major themes of John as they are given in the first and last chapters of his Gospel. Those themes will be interpreted by looking at stories in John's Gospel that demonstrate the meaning behind (or above) the text. The first four chapters of this volume unpack concepts from the epilogue of the Gospel. We will look at John 21:30-31 where John gives us his purpose for writing his Gospel. In the last four chapters we will unload the first chapter of John which contains the major themes of the Gospel and illustrates the significance of the stories as signs.

The next two volumes will continue to mine the nuggets uncovered by studying the structures of the text to show how the dialogues and events are signs pointing beyond themselves to the reality of the conflict between the *seen* and the *unseen* world. That conflict is represented in John's Gospel by the theme of *seeing and being seen*.

It is a joy to express my gratitude to those who have assisted in the process of writing and preparing the manuscript for publication. My wife, Lynda, spent many hours pouring over the early drafts of this book while fulfilling her other responsibilities as mother, grandmother, and friend to many. Patrick Selvey, a former student and friend, agreed to format the book and make it available to the public as an e-book. Eric Taylor, another former student and friend, also helped greatly in the early drafts of *Father's Love Journey*. His work was simply drafted into this new format. I would also like to express my gratitude to the many friends and students who encouraged me to make these insights available in print. They voiced their appreciation for the insights from John's Gospel as I taught it on college campuses; I now express my appreciation to them for their encouragement.

Chapter One

The Significance of Signs

John wrote his Gospel to produce a believing heart in his readers. His Gospel has held a special place in the heart of many since it was first published. It has indeed produced many believing hearts through the centuries. (The reason for the phrase "believing heart" rather than "faith" will be obvious as we continue.) It was written in remarkably simple language, yet it contains some of the most profound truths available in religious literature worldwide. Most people who reread this Gospel find something new each time they go through it.

John was writing for those who have a desire to see and experience more than information; for those who have a passion to dive deeper into the reality of who Jesus IS and to find a more intimate relationship with him. It was not written for those who were satisfied with their present level of life. *It was written for those who will never be satisfied with less than more.* No matter how deep you go in God, there is a deeper place in him. I want more than I found the first time I read this Gospel. I want a deeper relationship with him than I discovered while teaching it in colleges and churches for over 60 years.

My goal in this volume is to offer a hint for those who desire to plumb the depths of truth hidden in the text—not hidden from us but hidden for us to find. Parents often hide eggs during the Easter season. They do not hide them *from* their children; they hide them *for* their children to find. Parents rejoice when their children find the eggs. John hid some truths for us to find. He did not hide them from us. The mystery of the Gospel is in the nature of the reality John had experienced and which he wanted to communicate. As mystery it is both hidden and revealed at the same time. I think our Father finds more joy in our discovering those "hidden" truths than we experience when we find them.

John weaves various themes together through the fabric of his Gospel. We will look closely at several of them. Studying those themes is interesting and valuable, but they are not there for their own sake. They were not written to draw attention to themselves. The themes point beyond themselves to the hidden mystery. In themselves they are not the point. If I may borrow a phrase from a statement concerning John the Baptist, *these themes are not the light but bear witness to the light*. It is easy to get caught up in ideas and insights and miss the point.

The signs point to the mystery of *this man* who is the light of mankind, the light that shines upon and exposes every man and every woman. *This man* was (and is) a threat to those who hate the light. All John's signs illuminate the person and work of Jesus, the Son of God who is the light of the world for those who have eyes to see. John's stories help us see why our world system continually tries to suppress those who believe in him.

John's Purpose as Our Guide

John developed his Gospel with an explicit purpose. He wanted to challenge his readers to prove themselves to be believing disciples who receive life in the Father through Jesus the Son. That is an interesting fact because he was writing his Gospel to encourage those who had already believed on some level. He was not addressing the unbelievers. This ambiguity will dominate our thinking in this first section.

John 21:30-31 will be our guide here. The author spoke of himself as *"the disciple who is bearing witness to these things, and who has written these things"* (John 21:24). He also identified himself as *"the disciple whom Jesus loved"* (John 21:20). A witness is one who has seen with his own eyes and heard with his own ears. John wrote this testimony (Gospel) as an eyewitness. He was on the scene when the events took place. He saw with his own eyes and heard with his own ears (I John. 1:1). But he saw and heard beyond the obvious implications of what was said and what was done. He saw into the *unseen realm*; he saw what others had not seen.

This disciple obviously knew he had the same name as the John the Baptist. Like the Baptist, he did not come to bear witness to himself. That may be why he never mentioned his own name in his Gospel. Like the Baptist, he was not the Light, nor did he want to be in the limelight. His purpose was to point to the one he met when the Baptist pointed his finger and said, "Behold, the Lamb of God" (John 1:36). He wrote with the hope that his readers would follow his pointing quill and find something *hidden* in the one about whom he wrote, hidden from those whose eyes had not been opened to see the unseen realm. He wanted their blind eyes to be healed.

Our methodology will be to trace various themes in the Gospel considering John's purpose in writing: "*that you might believe*" (John 20:31). We will attempt to discover and uncover what John saw when he witnessed the words and acts as well as the tragedy and triumph of Jesus of Nazareth. He wrote this Gospel about 60 years after the events, so he had time to meditate and consider the implications of what happened to Jesus and through Jesus when he walked with his Father in the earth. What did John see? What did he want us to see? What did he want us to believe? These basic themes are outlined in John's explanation of why he wrote the Gospel.

A Metaphor for Believing

Since the concept of believing is central to John's purpose, we will consider the problems connected with believing before we attempt to uncover the truths hidden for us to find. This metaphor will help us.

Picture a teenage girl gazing at a boy with stars in her eyes. A cartoonist's imaginative balloon floats over her head. In that balloon bubbling up from her head stands a knight in shining armor. She does not see the young man who is standing in front of her; she sees a man who exists only in her imagination.

The picture in her balloon is her belief about the boy in front of her. Notice the connection between the image in her mind and her belief system. She believes him to be something he is not. But her belief does not change who he is.

Her image of the knight eclipses the real boy. If you try to convince her that the young man in front of her is nothing like the one in her mind's eye, you will discover how much power inner images have over what we believe and how we respond to life situations. Many fathers and mothers of teenagers know exactly what I am talking about. Reading John's Gospel will expose the balloons over the heads of the scribes and Pharisees. An imaginative picture of Jesus also hovered over the heads of the disciples as they followed him on his journey through the countryside of Israel. What was in their balloon influenced their responses to him. My balloon also influences my responses.

John's Purpose

With this metaphor in mind let us begin our study with the text in John 20:30-31. John wrote, *"Now Jesus did many other signs in the presence of the disciples which are not written in this book; but these are written that you may believe that Jesus is the Christ, the Son of God, and that believing you may have life in his name."* These phrases contain John's purpose in writing his Gospel. The major themes are stated clearly. We will unwrap these phrases one by one.

"These are written that you may believe." The reason John wrote this testimony was to invite his readers to see something in Jesus, something hidden from the eyes of many, and to believe in his name. We must see the whole of John's Gospel in terms of this

purpose. He did not leave us to guess what he wanted us to look for in his Gospel. He stated it very simply. He wanted his reader to see Jesus as the Christ, the Son of God. '*You*' includes all who read his testimony, even you and me today. Everything he recorded in his Gospel was to bring us to the place of seeing what he saw, hearing what he heard, and believing the way he believed.

However, as we look more closely at John's Gospel, we discover a concept of believing that is quite different from what most of us have in the balloon bubbling up from our head. This new way of understanding the notion of believing has formed and re-formed in my thinking through the many years I have spent meditating on and teaching the Gospel of John. The basic outline of the concept is as follows:

Biblical Believing

Believing is neither doctrinal nor biographical. It is *personal and relational.* John's purpose was not to describe the major details of Jesus' life accurately so that we might give mental ascent to their historical accuracy. He did give additional information about Jesus' life which is not in the other Gospels, but we have not yet seen what John was showing if we simply come away with more information. His concern was much deeper. The facts are there, and we can derive true doctrine from them if we leave our interpretive balloon behind. *The facts are not the light, they are there to bring us to the light*, to call us to believe, to connect us with the Father through Jesus the Son.

John was not trying to build a theology either. Theology can be extracted from the text, but all theology is at the mercy of the controlling opinion which the theologian brings with him or her to the text. There are almost as many interpretations of the text as there are scholars who have given their opinion of its meaning. Some interpretations are valuable; some are questionable. My interpretations are not exempt from this danger.

The real test of the value of any interpretation is whether the reader can personally *experience* the truth in Jesus as the Christ as they read the interpretation. The biblical text does not take the test; people who read it and interpret it do. The biblical text has passed the test of time. Each one of us takes that test again each time we read. Here is the test question: "Am I captivated, taken captive by Jesus? Am I bonding with him as I read, or am I merely receiving and processing information?" Without connecting and bonding to him, we have only the husk of truth. The kernel of the word-seed is missing. *Life is not in the husk; life is in the kernel.* That kernel is Jesus as the Christ, the Son of God. Not the doctrine; *this man*.

Definition

The root concept of the Greek word translated "believe" in John's Gospel implies being *taken in and held by* the compelling power of the one in whom we believe. It involves a personal commitment of oneself and all of one's resources to the one who first committed himself to mankind. In biblical believing, then, we are personally bound in a relationship by a covenant. We affirm this meaning of the word faith when we call a man *faithful* who honors his marriage covenant. He has made himself and his resources available to his covenant partner, his wife. When we believe in this biblical sense, we are *bound* to the one in whom we believe. God intended this deep bonding to be a normal part of human life because he created us for intimacy with him and with one another.

Believing, then, has everything to do with an intimate relationship. To believe in his name means to bond with him as a follower, as a disciple of the one who bears the name Jesus. But there is more. Jesus said to believe in him was to believe in the Father who sent him (John 12:44). Jesus wants us to enter an intimate relationship with his Father. To commit to the Son is to commit to his Father. When we are bonded to the Son we are bonded to the Father because the Father and the son are one. We are also bonded to the community of believers when we believe in this sense (John 17:22).

So, the concept of believing is more than a commitment of your mind to a doctrine; it is the experience of your whole person being taken into and held by the personal God and his way of doing life. It is also being taken into the community with the commission Jesus gave his disciples. The faithful Son of God gave his life in love to his creation. He then called for faithful followers who willingly and lovingly give their lives to him as partners in a life of receiving Father's love and giving it away to others.

The Content of Belief

"*That Jesus is the Christ.*" John sought to offer a very definite object to which the believer will be bound. John was saying, "The Christ of God whom the Father promised is *this man* Jesus and I want you to allow him to bind you to *himself*, to his *community* and to his *mission*." Believing in Jesus as the Christ means giving yourself to him and to the community of believers for the sake of *his Father's mission* in the earth. It is all about bonding to a unique *person* with a unique *community* and a unique *mission*. That mission is to reconcile the world to Father's love.

John was not asking us to ascribe to some doctrinal system built around a concept of Christ which men have conceived in their balloon (like the girl in our metaphor). He was not interested in the ideas and concepts of the leading theologians of his day. His concern was that we might see Christ in *this man* Jesus. John wanted us to recognize Jesus and receive him as the Son of the Father. He wanted us to be apprehended by *this man*. That is why he wrote. That is why he called his writing a testimony. He testified to things he had seen and heard to bring others to see what he had seen. He wanted his readers to be grasped by the Christ who is Jesus and to become participants in his mission.

To say this in a negative way, John was not writing a biography, at least not in the sense that we have biographies today. We can understand his Gospel best if we think of it as a sermon. Preaching is designed to call people to a commitment to the person of Jesus as the Christ. A preacher chooses stories that illustrate the points of his sermon. The chronological sequence of what happened is less important in preaching than the point the preacher is trying to get across. He may choose to relate the stories in a different order from the way they happened because he uses the stories to point beyond themselves to a reality beyond the stories. John's Gospel is like that.

The stories in John's Gospel point to a reality beyond our mental capacity to grasp. But although we cannot grasp them, he to whom the signs point can grasp us if we leave our balloons behind and watch the story unfold before us. We must allow the stories to grab us and take us where they are going. This is what Paul meant when he said he would press on to get ahold of (grasp) that which Christ had in his mind when he got ahold of (grasped) him (Phil. 3:12). Paul had been apprehended by Jesus who is the Christ. He wanted to apprehend that for which he was apprehended.

A Person With a History

The content of John's theology is a person. The Christ is not an idea or a doctrine about an office. This person has a history. His history did not begin at his birth, not even in Mary's womb. He was the *Logos* of God in the beginning with God and this *Logos* was God (John 1:1). He is eternally in the bosom of the Father (John 1:18). He had already been involved in this world before he came in the flesh. "*All things were made through him*" (John 1:2). Nor did his *coming* begin at the birth of Jesus. "*He was always coming into the world*" (John 1:9).

This Eternal Word came out from the bosom of the Father into our world of flesh (John 1:14). He dwelt among us (the word 'dwell' is a verb form of the word for 'tent'). The Eternal Word of God *pitched his tent in our camp*. This is a picture drawn from what happened in the wilderness after the Exodus. Moses built a Tabernacle (tent) and the glory of God's presence descended and took up residence in that tent. God pitched his tent in Israel's camp and went with them as he led them to the Promised Land. In Jesus as the Christ, the Word of God pitched his tent in our camp and is going with us toward the coming kingdom of God in the earth. This is an example of John's *midrashic* method of telling stories that point beyond themselves to a reality beyond words.

We must see the details of *this man's* life considering where he came from and where he was going. *His life and ministry were all about the bosom of the Father.* If we do not find the Father when we believe in Jesus, we have not yet believed in him for who he is (John. 14:9). He was in the Father and the Father was in him. To find him—to find who he really is—is to find the Father of glory who was the inner, *unseen* reality of *this man* Jesus whose flesh was the 'tent' in which his *unseen* Father dwelt.

Just as Christ's coming did not begin with his birth, so also his life did not end with his death. He is still with us today. He is still coming to his people daily. He does not leave us desolate; he comes to us and walks with us as we follow him. We as a Body are the Sanctuary (tent) in which God's Spirit dwells and moves about in our world today (I Cor. 3:16). He is leading his people through history toward the consummation of the ages when he will reconcile "all thing to himself, whether on earth or in heaven" (Col. 1:20). John in his Gospel is calling us to be a part of that work of reconciliation of the world to Christ.

Any reading of John that fails to keep these things in view falls short of John's purpose. The readings of John presented in this book are not exempt. They also fall short. I have not yet fully seen what John saw. *We can only bear witness to what we have seen.* Like Paul, we know in part and we prophesy (or teach) in part (I Cor. 13:9). Too many leaders bear witness to what theologians and preachers have said. They have not yet seen with their own eyes or heard with their own ears. Hearsay is not admitted in a court of law.

The Person Defines the Name

Jesus is the one John presented for us to observe. He is the one John wanted us to believe in. John's message to his contemporaries was: "The Christ for whom you wait is *this man* Jesus. The one who was promised has come; his name is Jesus. You have believed in the promise, now believe in the one who was promised. He is *this man*, Jesus. *This is the man (ecce homo)*. He is the Christ."

We are not at liberty to supply the meaning of the title *Christ* from our own understanding, to project onto Jesus our ideas of what the Christ *ought* to be. Our interpretation of the promise does not define the title. We simply look to *this man* Jesus and see in him the Christ. The title *Christ* derives its meaning from the person and work of *this man*; it is not the other way around. Jesus did not derive his meaning from any preconceived notion even if that image is found in the Old Testament. We may have interpreted those texts according to our preconceived notions.

In other words, no matter how lofty our concepts may be or how eloquently we speak, the reality of who he *IS* trumps our ideas and overrides the words we use to talk about him. He is Lord over our imagination. The problem comes when we have a picture in our mind's eye while telling others how Jesus affected us when we believed. If our image of him does not correspond to the reality of who he is, we may lead others to believe in the Jesus in our balloon rather than in him. The disciples had that same difficulty during Jesus' earthly life. They saw him through their colored glasses. When he came under the judgment of the High Priest, they did not know what to do. They proved themselves to be what I call *unbelieving believers on their way to believing.*

His Identity

"*The Son of God.*" Many ideas also orbited around the title *Son of God*. Kings and emperors often presented themselves as sons of the gods. People of those days also thought of angels as sons of God in some sense. However, we cannot define Jesus in terms of some philosophical or theological notion of a Son of God whether in the first century or today. John gave details of the life of *this man* Jesus to define the title. Again, this can never be reversed by using some humanistic concept to define Jesus' identity as the Son of God.

We learn what *Son of God* means by reading what was written about *this man*. If we try to project the image of our fantasy image onto Jesus, like the girl in our metaphor did with her knight in shining armor, we will never see him for who he really is. We might say John has written these things to pop our balloons. It will be unfortunate if our balloons do not pop before we face him in the final Day.

In the sections that follow we will look at some events of Jesus' life seeking to open our view to what is beyond the external details, what is *unseen* by the natural eye. Our goal will be to discover the Jesus John wrote about. Our goal is to pursue the way he walked, recognizing that some preach *"another Jesus,"* a *"different spirit"* and a *"different gospel"* (II Cor. 11:4). We are not looking for one who conforms to our mental images, nor are we simply seeking more information about the one we think we know. We want to see the one John was pointing to with the stories he recorded. *This man Jesus is alive, and he is here today ready to make himself known to you from his place in Father's bosom.*

We may deflate some balloons as we try to understand John's Gospel. Many of my own false images decomposed during my personal study of this Gospel over a period of many years, some disintegrated even as I was writing these meditations. I have been on this journey long enough to expect that more of my ideas will come under the spotlight after this volume is published, but I have learned to welcome with gratitude each challenge as it comes. I am under no illusion that I am always right or that I have arrived at ultimate truth. I only know in part (I Cor. 13:9).

The Goal of Believing

The leading hermeneutic in these reflections comes from what Jesus said when Philip asked to see the Father. Jesus said, *"Whoever has seen me, has seen the Father"* (John 14:9). Philip had been looking *at* Jesus, but he had not yet seen the *unseen* side of what he was looking at. He was looking through his mental filter. If we do not see the Father, we have not yet seen Jesus for who he IS. We will not find ultimate fulfillment if we merely see historical details about his life and teaching. In seeing Jesus, we want to see the Father. In looking *at* Jesus through John's stories, we are looking *for* the Father. Jesus wants us to *see through him* to his Father. The *unseen* Father can only be seen through the medium of the Jesus we *see*, and then only if our eyes have been washed in the pool of Siloam (John 9).

"T*hat believing you may have life in his name.*" Some surprises are in store for those who have never looked carefully at John's development of this theme of believing. Remember though, the theme is not there for itself. We are looking for the one in whom we are to believe, the one with whom we are to bond, the one who wants to captivate us. And we want to understand how to experience the kind of believing that brings us into an intimate relationship with the Father who was and is present to the world in Jesus Christ. In relating to him and believing in him we receive life. With that life we also receive the commission and the ability to love the world as he loves.

Levels of Believing

We will discover different levels of believing in John's Gospel. There is a believing that brings life: "*He who believes in the Son has eternal life*" (John 3:36). He who experiences this kind of believing will not be condemned (John 3:18) and will be raised up in the last day (John 6:40). However, there is also a believing to which Jesus will not commit himself. "*Many believed in his name when they saw the signs which he did; but Jesus did not trust himself to them*" (John 2:23-24). There is a critical distinction. Those who desire all that God made available in Christ Jesus must make sure their believing is of the first category.

Jesus will not trust himself to us as believers if we are only bonded to our *concept* of the Messiah. There is no value in pursuing a relationship with him through that kind of believing. He will not adjust himself to our belief system; we must adjust our belief system to him. Our focus must shift from "trusting Jesus" to the more radical question, "*Does he trust himself to me?*"

We can detect a transition from one level of believing to another in several of John's stories. In the healing of the nobleman's son, for example, the man "*believed the word that Jesus spoke,*" but later it is said of him that "*he himself believed*" (John 4:46-54). The difference between the first and the second believing is not clear in that text, but something extra is obviously implied in the second believing. Something happened in the nobleman's life which brought him to the next level of believing. His servants reported that his son was healed the same hour Jesus had spoken his creative word. When he heard that report, he was confronted with reality, not just a word.

There are also negative examples. To the Jews who had believed in him, Jesus said, "*If you* live by [abide in] *my word, you are truly my disciples, and you will* experience [know] *the truth, and the truth will make you free*" (John 8:31-32). Notice the "if". The Jews had believed in him and were being offered a chance to become his disciples. There are conditions to becoming a disciple beyond believing. In other words, simply believing does not make you a disciple. True disciples are those who abide in and live by his word. It is they who are made free.

The Jews who believed in him were not willing to admit their bondage: "*We are sons of Abraham and have never been in bondage to anyone*" (John 8:33). In their minds they *were* free; they needed no liberation. Jesus did not make himself or his resources available to those who thought they were already free. This concept appears in the other Gospels when Jesus said he did not come for the well but for the sick. He did not come for the righteous but for the sinners.

In the text that follows, John made it clear that the Jews who had believed were not on the path to life even though they had believed in him. They believed in the Christ of their preconceived notions rather than the Christ who was offering them freedom. Jesus even went so far as to say they were worshiping the wrong God (John 8:44). They were on the wrong track from the beginning. To continue running on that track would be to miss him completely.

So much for the *nature* of believing. Now we move to the *goal* of believing.

Chapter Two

The Goal of Believing

As we pursue this theme through various texts, we will receive direction from the words Jesus cried out after his triumphal entry: "*He who believes in me, believes not in me but in him who sent me*" (John 12:24). At first there appears to be a contradiction: "He who believes in me believes not in me." The point is that the goal of believing is to be joined to the Father through the Son. If we have believed in Jesus without coming into an abiding relationship with his Father, we have not yet effectively believed in Jesus.

The Pharisees were looking for a Messiah who only existed in the imagination of their heart. Their Messiah was not the Son of the Father. In their mind, God could not have a human Son. We will live a life of continual disappointment if our expectations are based on false images of Christ. Life issues from what is in the imagination of our hearts. It is a fact that the imagination of man's heart was on evil continually which invited Noah's flood (Gen. 6:5).

Since believing in Jesus is ultimately believing in the one who sent him, we have not reached the goal of believing if we have not yet come to the Father. When we come to Jesus, we have come to him who is the way to the Father (John 14:6). *Jesus is the way; the bosom of the Father is the destination.* In our journey through

John's Gospel we will discover that we do not have to wait till we die to be in Father's bosom. Father's loving embrace is available now.

Preconceived Notions

One key to understanding John's Gospel is tied to this concept of preconceived notions. A preconceived notion is an idea or an expectation we bring with us into a situation. It is the mental picture of a thing before we see the thing itself. It is like a dream, but more dangerous because *it changes the way we see the real thing* when it is there in front of us. We see what we expect to see, not necessarily what is there. When we dream, we eventually wake up and realize it was only a dream, but with a preconceived notion we do not know we are dreaming.

When we are under the influence of preconceived notions, we have a form of mental blindness. Philosophers call this blindness *cognitive bias*. It is the most serious kind of blindness because we think we see clearly. *There are none as blind as those who refuse to look because they think they already see.* They never seek confirmation outside themselves. That was the problem of the girl in our cartoon metaphor in chapter one. If she protects her picture of the knight in shining armor too carefully, she may end up married to a man she does not know and does not even like.

In Jesus' day the Jewish people had traditional ideas about the coming Messiah. They brought those concepts and expectations with them into their encounter with Jesus. Their ideas were based on the study of Scripture and their national history. They had very orthodox reasons for expecting the Messiah of their balloon, but their image was nothing like the real Messiah who stood in front of them. They knew exactly what they were looking for in a Messiah, but they were looking for the wrong Messiah. When Jesus refused to conform to their preconceived notions, they plotted to kill him and continued to look for the Messiah of their dreams. Since their idea of Messiah was false, they were expecting a false Messiah.

A Human Problem

This is not a Jewish problem; *it is a human problem*. We Christians also have concepts of Christ based on our study of the Bible and our denominational history. We fill our theological balloons with what we consider to be orthodox ideas backed up by convincing arguments just like the Pharisees did. Like them we also use our devotional life to prove our piety and we use our good deeds to proclaim our holiness. We may even claim the presence of Christ among us when we are together. Like the Pharisees, some of us like to expose the "heretics" who disagree with us. We want to destroy their reputation and get others to join us in rejecting them as well. That is not the Holy Spirit; it is an unholy, divisive spirit.

In all this activity the question arises: If Jesus himself were to appear in our midst, would he trust himself and his resources to us? Would we recognize him? Would our expectations allow us to see him for who he really is? Are you certain? *Pharisees are always certain.*

Modern Idolatry

Idolatry in our culture takes the form of preconceived notions. We do not mold clay, wood or metal to reflect our image of God but, just like the crowd in John 6, we try to pressure Christ to become the king we picture in our minds rather than allowing him to be the king he IS. Our contrived mental images control our responses to him. It matters little that these images are not in stone; they are still part of that mythical, demonic world where the gods are merely extensions of our rebellious human imagination (Gen. 6:5).

Our knowledge of Christ is invalid to the extent that we have false images of him. *"Claiming to be wise, they turned out to be fools, and exchanged the glory of the immortal God for images resembling death bound man..."* (Rom. 1:22–23). If we stubbornly cling to the images we hold in our mind's eye, we are in danger of exchanging the glory of Christ for our human image of him. We end up relating to a Christ who can do nothing for us because he exists only in our imagination. The Christ who cannot do anything in our world today is a false Christ. The real Christ did not leave his doctor's bag or his psychiatrist's couch in the first century. He can and does heal, deliver, and bring reconciliation today.

The Effect on Church Life

People often enter churches expecting God to do great things for them. Like the crowd in John 6:66 they walk away when they realize the church is not doing things their way. *Thinking they have seen clearly; they have not seen at all.* In their private religious enterprise, they become *church hoppers* in search of the church of their dreams. Too many Don-Quixote-Christians are chasing figments of their imagination. One can only hope and pray they become disillusioned and open themselves to an encounter with the Christ who is Jesus. In Miguel de Cervantes' novel, Don Quixote does not become disillusioned until his death when he experiences a conversion of sorts. Hopefully, we will become disillusioned sooner than that.

There are others who seek the reality they read about in the Scriptures. When they see contemporary congregations reflecting the world system more than the image of Christ, they become discouraged and begin to look for him in a life apart from the Church. I rejoice that there are many congregations today that participate in advancing the kingdom of God in the earth. But there are too many that are sadly little more than the extension of the pastor's theological opinion. This causes some to walk away who are genuinely desiring a relationship with God.

My prayer is that more and more Christians, me included, will forsake their illusions, and have a fresh, daily encounter with the true Christ so we, the Church, can give an effective witness to the world. *None of us has an image of God that perfectly reflect the reality of who he is.* Our pilgrimage must become a process of receiving fresh revelation each day. When we allow the veil of our preconceived notions to be torn, *"beholding his glory with unveiled face"* we will begin the process of being changed into the likeness of what we see (II Cor. 3:17).

Our problem is not mental images; we all have them. God created us with an imaging faculty because he desires to fill it with himself through dreams, visions, and insights. All of us have ideas in our heart of hearts that are based on what we have been taught or what we have imagined to be true. We also have many pictures in our imagination that are true because we have experienced God personally. *The problem comes when we fiercely refuse to consider the possibility that some of our mental pictures of Christ may be wrong or at least misleading.*

John Speaks to the Problem

John's Gospel is unique among the Gospels, as we have noticed. Understanding this uniqueness helps unlock the meaning of the stories and teachings presented in his Gospel. As we read John we must continually ask, "Why did John record the life of Jesus so differently from the other Gospels?" It is not enough to notice that it is different; we must discern the *significance* of these differences. To what do the differences point?

John had a twofold purpose. First, he was calling the religious people of the first century to abandon their mental image of Christ. Second, he called them to follow Jesus to the bosom of the Father. His Gospel also calls the church of every age to forsake their images, recognize Jesus as the Christ, the Son of God, and follow Jesus into the Father's presence. Jesus is himself the way to the Father. In what follows I will *not* be trying to draw a better picture of Jesus for you to carry in your mental backpack. I will simply challenge you to seek and follow the Jesus who *"is in the bosom of the Father"* (John 1:18).

He made our journey into Father's bosom possible when he disarmed the principalities and powers—those gods who reign in the domain of our rebellious imagination (Col. 2:15). Those powers try to control the space between ourselves and the true God. Jesus made a way for us to walk through enemy territory into our Father's presence. We can follow this way only as we let Jesus reveal himself to us by the Spirit and replace our favorite images with the living Jesus, the true image of the invisible God.

True Disciples

A disciple is one who follows a teacher and learns from him how to live life. Some of the rabbis of Jesus' day were more interested in showing their disciples how to live life as a Jew than they were in leading them into a relationship with God. That is no different than Christian leaders who are more interested in making "good Baptists" or "good Catholics" than helping their people develop an intimate relationship with God. Our goal in this section is to pursue the basic question of discipleship: What does it mean to follow "Rabbi Jesus" who is the Way? We can ask this in two different ways:

We can ask, "What does it mean to *follow* Jesus?

Or we can ask, "What does it mean to follow *Jesus*?"

With the emphasis on *our following*, we can follow the imaginary Jesus in our mental backpack rather than Jesus himself. This can look like true discipleship, especially to others who have the same false image we have. That is really an exercise in unbelief. It is a work of man apart from God's presence. It is an exercise in *unbelief* (or it is belief in *another Jesus*) because the object of that faith is the Jesus of our imagination. Paul warned us about this danger of this other Jesus (II Cor. 11:4).

If there is another Jesus, a different spirit, and a different gospel, valid questions arise: Which gospel am I believing? Which Jesus am I following? Which spirit motivates and empowers me? True faith and true discipleship can only follow the *authentic Jesus as he really IS—yesterday, today, and forever.*

Yet true disciples will *follow* Jesus. How could it be discipleship otherwise? The possibility of following a false Jesus does not relieve us of the responsibility to follow. If I stumble in my attempt to follow (and I do), I do not backslide. I fall toward Jesus since I am walking forward with him and toward him, not away from him. You might say I *"frontslide"* when I fail.

Jesus Is the Way

To follow implies the two of you are going somewhere. Here again we come face to face with Jesus himself. He said, *"I am the way, and the truth, and the life; no one comes to the Father, but by me"* (John 14:6). The way is not a path we can follow apart from the presence of Jesus because he is himself the way. *Jesus in you is his way for you.*

A way has a goal, a destination. In this case both the way and the destination are in Jesus Christ who is in the bosom of the Father

(John 1:18). The goal is to be in the Father's embrace. Jesus is in the Father. You cannot get any closer than that. So, to be in Christ is to be held in the Father's loving embrace. Here is one of the many paradoxes of John's Gospel: To be in Christ is to be at rest *in the Father's bosom* and to follow Jesus is to be *on the way* to the Father's bosom. We are called to be at rest in Jesus Christ as we move with him toward the fulfillment of his mission in the earth.

As we develop the themes of John's Gospel, we will keep before us three basic truths. First is the absolute uniqueness of *this man* Jesus. Second is the uniqueness of *the way he walked*. And third, we will remain alert to the truth that *he is walking among us today as well*.

Words and Images

In approaching this issue, I am aware of the dilemma we face with words and images. *Words create images*. If I say "cat" you automatically picture a cat in your mind. But the cat in your mind might be quite different from the cat I am talking about. You may have a picture in your mind of a big white fluffy cat while I am thinking of a little yellow tabby. To be certain we have the same cat in mind, the cat I am referring to must be there so I can point and say, "This cat." John wants to point us to "*This Man*" Jesus.

The only way any of us can be sure others see Jesus when we are speaking of him is if Jesus Christ shows up for the person we are talking to. This introduces another complication: if I talk about Jesus who is present to me (yet *unseen*), the audience can still be thinking of the Jesus of their childhood Sunday school lesson. If they have not matured in their personal relationship with Jesus, true words can still miss the mark. That is exactly what was happening in the first century when Jesus was speaking to the Pharisees. His audience had pictures in their minds that were different from the Jesus standing in front of them (*seen*) speaking words about himself and his Father (*unseen*).

Here is our problem. On the one hand, *we use words*. The concepts and images in your mind might be, probably are, different from those in mine. On the other hand, *we must use words* to present (the *unseen*) Jesus Christ because there is no other way to present him. Well, that is not quite true. There is no other way to present him in a book. We present a picture of him every day with our lives if we are really walking with him. We are like little incarnate words to the degree that we portray (the *unseen*) Jesus with our love, grace, hope, and peace. The *unseen* becomes *seeable* through us.

Whether by words or by actions, we cannot present him to you in the same way he was present to the disciples in his day. He is not here physically. He is unseen. We can only use words and actions to point and indicate the direction to look. You may turn *inwardly* to see the one of whom we speak, or you may not turn. My choice is to write, it is up to you, the reader, to follow the pointing finger of my presentation.

Our Method: Watching His Walk

In the following meditations we will not deal with all the themes of John, but only those that relate to the question of discipleship and its goal: "What does it mean to follow *this man* Jesus and to walk in the same way he walked? How can we experience the Father's embrace and make his love known to the world?"

In unfolding key words and phrases, we will refer to various stories and dialogues in the Gospel, but not in the order they appear. I am taking this approach because of John's style. He introduced a theme in one place and developed it in different ways through other stories and dialogues throughout his Gospel.

Chapter Three
The Significance of Signs

This section will focus on John 20:30. We saw in verse 31 *why* John wrote: "That you may believe." Here we find *what* he wrote. "*Now Jesus did many other signs in the presence of the disciples which are not written in this book.*" John wrote signs. He did not write *about* signs; he wrote signs. Keep this in mind as we continue.

"*Now Jesus did many other signs....*" The key word here is *signs*. Understanding what John meant by this term opens the way to understanding what John was saying through the stories and dialogues of his Gospel. The Scriptures refer to the supernatural deeds of Jesus in three ways: miracles, wonders, and signs.

Miracle refers to the power necessary to accomplish the deed.

Wonder draws attention to the response of amazement on the part of those who witness the deed.

Sign draws attention to the fact that the deed points beyond itself. In other words, the *deed* does not merely *accomplis*h something, it *means* something. The only proper response to a sign is to find out what it is pointing to and to follow the arrow until you find the thing itself.

If I were on a long trip and got hungry, it would be foolish to stop and try to eat a sign advertising a restaurant. I need the sign to find what I am looking for but having located the sign I have not yet arrived at the restaurant. My goal is to find food and eat. If I am too impressed with the sign and stop to analyze the artwork, I am in danger of missing the thing to which it points. If I am too impressed with the language and cultural background of the Gospel, I may miss the meal it offers—the (*unseen*) Bread of Life.

The Pointing Finger

One of my sons helped me see this when he was in middle school. I asked him to carry out the trash as I pointed toward the door. "Dad," he exclaimed with excitement as he took my pointing finger in his hand, "I just learned that the number of hairs between the knuckles of the finger are inherited. Look, Dad. You're almost bald between the second and third knuckle; and so am I." An accurate observation, but the trash had not moved. He had noticed details about the pointing finger, but he neglected the *meaning* of the pointing finger. He had *seen* the hairs on my finger, but not trash.

We all do the same thing with the Scriptures sometimes. Many Bible teachers and interpreters spend years analyzing the text without ever following the sign to discover the person the Scripture speaks of. Many believers are impressed with teachers who analyze the texts, identify all the Greek words, and explain all the cultural and historical background. Yet their lives remain unaffected by the most obvious command: "Love one another." They argue and fight over *doctrines* that amount to *nothing more than splitting the hairs between the knuckles of the pointing finger*. I have personally participated in many of those kinds of arguments only to wake up and realize I had been living in my theological balloon again.

When John the Baptist pointed and said, "Behold, the Lamb of God," we do not want to begin counting the number of hairs between the knuckles of his finger. We want to follow the direction of the finger and find the Jesus he is pointing to. To follow the pointing finger of the Gospel, we sometimes need to consider the Greek words and cultural background. But those things are not the point. They are only indications of the direction we must face as we seek the Father whose love is present in Jesus.

More Than Miracles

We usually think of *signs* as being about Jesus' miracles and wonders. Miracles are indeed signs, but John was thinking of all the acts and sayings of Jesus when he spoke of the many signs Jesus did. The cleansing of the Temple was as much a sign for John as the changing of the water to wine. When Jesus stooped to the ground and forgave the woman caught in adultery, that was also a sign for John. All the acts and statements in the Gospel were signs pointing beyond themselves to a reality found in Jesus and his relationship with his Father. All signs were designed to point to and draw the reader into the Father's loving embrace.

John recorded these signs so we readers might find a pointer leading us to a reality beyond our imaginative picture to the reality John himself had seen with his eyes and touched with his hands (I

John 1:1). When we come to the reality to which the signs point, we will believe, we will join the Son in the Father and become sons and daughters of God. We will also join the Father's mission and channel his love to the world.

John chose the signs he recorded for a reason. From the many signs, John chose these because they would bring readers who follow the pointing finger to life in Jesus as the Christ. As we begin to look for life in his name, *we are seeking*. We are already on the way to the reality to which the sign point. But if we are merely looking for more historical information, we are in danger of missing the point and floundering in our attempt to know the Father.

Approaching the stories as signs does not deny their historical value. But seeing the stories as signs is infinitely more valuable because the reward is life in his name. The goal of seeking is to find life, real life in the bosom of the Father. More information may be of historical and cultural value; the meaning of the Greek words may have value for our academic advancement. But what John wanted us to see is of more value than all the academic information in the hundreds of volumes of commentaries. Our cry is simple, "*We would see Jesus*" (John. 12:21).

Events and Stories

It will help if we make another distinction before we develop this thought. The way the signs were available to John is quite different from the way they are available to us. Jesus was there in the flesh for John. For us he is there in the stories. I do not say that he is there *only* in the stories. He is really in the stories for those who have eyes to see the unseen. He is *there* because he is *here* whether you read the story or not.

He went away, but he promised to come again in a form the world would not see (John 14:19). Today he comes to those who have received him, who have believed in his name. He really is here, and he can manifest himself to us as we read the text with a willingness for him to dissolve our false images and pop our balloons.

When I first started studying the gospel stories, I thought it would have been more exciting to be alive in those days. "It would have been easier to get to know him then," I mused. As we continue our study, we will see that it was not any easier for those who saw him in the flesh than it is for us who see him in and through the stories. Most of the Pharisees never saw through his physical presence to the *unseen realm.*

The Father was available to them in the presence of Jesus in the flesh, but many missed him. *Father is available to us in the presence of Jesus Christ in the stories.* We sometimes miss him because we get caught up in the stories without following the line of the pointing finger. In either case, whether in the actual events or in the text that witnesses to those events, only the Spirit can reveal the real presence of the Father in the person of Jesus the Christ.

Those of Jesus' day needed to follow the arrow of the *events*. We must follow the arrow of the *stories*. The Pharisees got hung up in the external details of the events because Jesus did not fit the images in their minds. They saw Jesus working miracles but still failed to recognize him for who he was. Even the disciples had trouble following the line of the signs until after the resurrection and outpouring of the Holy Spirit.

We do not want to get hung up in the external details of the stories and miss the person who is present but unseen. The arrow can be followed in either case, that is, in an actual event or in a story, only by the Spirit. But it can be followed. We must follow it if we desire to experience the fellowship of the Father and the Son by the Spirit.

Application to Bible Study

Let us develop this thought now. If John, the disciple whom Jesus loved, was writing these stories as signs, then it behooves us to follow the line indicated by the stories just as one would follow the arrow on a sign advertising a restaurant.

John would be disappointed that some of us today are satisfied with learning new details about the earthly life of Jesus. Our human tendency is to prefer concepts that we can control and facts we can interpret as we see fit. Are we avoiding a personal relationship with the Father because we cannot control that relationship? Do we prefer a relationship with a text over a relationship with a living God who is a loving Father? Are we caught up in the signs pointing to the feast and failing to come to the table spread before us?

It is much easier to *talk* about having a relationship than to *be in* one. We are more comfortable with external details of the stories because those details require nothing of us, like boys who talk about relationships with girls but are afraid to face a real girl. In this way we can maintain the illusion that we are in a relationship. Preferring a fantasy world where we can control all the characters, we have the feelings of a relationship without having to face the real Christ. It is easy to get bogged down in details for their own sake when we focus on the text. That was the tendency of much of the scholarship of the eighteenth and nineteenth centuries and into the twentieth.

For example, scholars spent much time and effort trying to determine which tomb in Jerusalem is the actual place where Jesus was buried. There is historical value in such studies. But even if we could prove which place was the actual burial site, we would only be able to notice that the grave is empty. *We already knew that.* Nor is it enough to stand in wonder and amazement at the fact that he is not there. We would do better to join Mary as she lingered around until the risen Lord appeared.

The stories have not had their intended effect until we experience his presence and worship him as our Lord and our God. *Shall we linger together?*

We can spend our lives studying the original languages and the historical and cultural background and still be totally unprepared to approach the text with eyes that see him. I know because I have done that. Having learned to use the various tools for Bible study, I was able to analyze a text and produce an exegetical masterpiece which was accurate in terms of linguistic and cultural background. But in all that effort for many years I had missed the point.

We must learn from the rabbis of Jesus' day. They knew the Scriptures better than any scholar of our day, yet many of them missed the person the Scriptures were pointing to. They were looking at the external trappings of the life of Jesus and interpreting them based on their preconceived notions. They did not see the signs as signs. They did not follow the arrow to find rest in the bosom of the Father. If it was possible for them to miss the point, it is also possible for us.

Theology and Biography

The word *sign* indicates that John was not focused on biography but on the real-life implications of *this man's* life, death, and resurrection. In this Gospel, John was trying to orient us to the Father in the events in the life of Jesus and to show how we can *join him in the bosom of the Father.*

For example, John was not so much interested in the fact that Jesus fed the multitude with only five loaves and two fish. It was a miracle and a wonder, but the miracle was not his point. He wanted us to ask, "What does this mean?" He wanted us to *discover and partake* of the "Bread of Life" not just to articulate an accurate doctrine of Jesus as the Bread of Life. John's focus was on *pointing*.

Once I was presenting this concept and a student challenged the notion that John is more interested in pointing than biography. He had been exposed to a theology that limited the Gospels to their biographical elements. Like so many in our day, he equated theology with academic intellectualizing of the gospel. There is a theology that presents the gospel in philosophical terms, speaking as though it were nothing more than a series of doctrinal propositions or biographical details to be affirmed or denied. But that is not true biblical theology. It is only human philosophy in theological clothing.

That way of humanizing the Bible may be what prompted John to write his first letter. Some Greek intellectuals of his later years tried to explain the life of Jesus Christ in terms of their philosophy, a philosophy that later came to be known as Gnosticism. They used the stories of Jesus' life as signs, but they were pointing to the Christ of their preconceived notions. They even made up a few stories of their own because the stories that came down through the disciples who knew him personally could not easily point in the direction of their false Christ. John almost certainly had these philosophers in mind when he said, "*...many antichrists have come*" (I John. 2:18).

Paul addressed a similar situation when he warned about those who preach "another Jesus" and offer "a different spirit" (II Cor. 11:4). The true Christ never fits into the cognitive bias of humanistic intellectuals. On the other hand, the spirit of antichrist will gladly enter your biased imagery and draw you away from the pointing finger of the signs in John's Gospel.

Failure to Follow the Signs

My response to the student's challenge was to draw attention to the real problem. The failure to see the Gospel from its pointing perspective is the very thing that leads to such philosophical nonsense. Theology is words that point in the direction other words; *words about words about God are only words and more words.* Whether it is good theology or bad theology depends on the direction the arrow is pointing. *Wrong words point in the wrong direction.* False theological structures produce false concepts.

One can even use all the proper terminology and still miss the point. Even speaking the right words (as though there were right words) and pointing in the right direction does not guarantee the hearers will get the point. Jesus used all the right words and pointed in the right direction, but many did not see because they were listening through the grid of their mental images.

Chapter Four

Disciples and Presence

This brings us to the critical point we began with. When we approach the life of Jesus with preconceived notions based on our own human understanding apart from a personal encounter with the *unseen*, we will only see what our training has programmed us to see. The believing that comes from such seeing is a believing produced by blindness. Jesus did not entrust himself to this kind of believing. Jesus did not show himself to the Pharisees who thought they could see, but he did show himself to the blind man who admitted his blindness and received his sight (John 9).

Our next discussion begins with the statement: "...*In the presence of the disciples*" (John 20:30). We will look at the implications of the word *disciple* before we turn to the question of presence. The word *disciple* represents another major theme in John's Gospel. Just like there were surprises in the context of believing, so there are surprises here for those who have not yet followed John's way of presenting different levels of discipleship.

A disciple is one who follows a teacher to discover how to live life. Many of Jesus' disciples drew back when he did not do what they expected. They no longer followed him. These obviously were not true disciples. There were also the few who followed him until he was arrested. How could they be called disciples since they forsook him? Yet John calls both groups disciples. And there were the two who followed him to his trial. One of those, Peter, denied him there. Was Peter still a disciple? Yes! Somehow! But how is he different? Only one, the disciple whom Jesus loved, followed him all the way to the cross. Was he more of a disciple or a better disciple than the others? Are we comparing ourselves to ourselves?

Disciples and Their Dreams

If a disciple is one who follows (and that is the biblical definition of the term) then the multitude could be called "*un-disciples*" since they only followed while he was going the way they thought the Messiah should go. They were the '*unbelieving believers*' to whom Jesus would not commit himself. He would not trust himself to them because they were not really following him; *they were following their Dream-Christ.*

These *un-disciples* were merely excited because they thought they had found in Jesus the fulfillment of their messianic dreams. He was their *knight in shining armor.* As Jesus continued to go the way his Father set before him, they saw that their messianic ideals were in opposition to the way he was walking. They chose to follow their dreams and leave Jesus behind. "*Will you also go away?*" he asked the twelve (John 6:67). Love does not control; it freely offers and waits for a response.

A serious question rises at this point. What is a true disciple? How far and in what sense does one have to follow before he or she is really a disciple? How much failure is allowed before one is exposed as an *un-disciple*? Judas followed all the way to the last night but was shown to be the betrayer. As it turned out, the disciples who ran away in the night were still disciples in the end, somehow or other. Peter became the chief of the apostles even though he is the one who denied him.

True Disciples

According to this view, a true disciple is one who follows Jesus to find the Father in the Son and the Son in the Father. A true disciple also joins in the peaceful life of God on his way through their action into the hearts of the present generation. So, discipleship consists of following Jesus as the Way into his Father's bosom. The Father is the destination. There are degrees of entering this peaceful life; one can be more-or-less in—*less in is still in*. There are times of being in and times of being on the periphery. But if we have not entered the Way into fellowship with the Father, we have not yet begun to experience the fullness of what is available to every true disciple. If we are moving in that direction and advancing in that relationship, we are still disciples even when we fail.

The Problem of Presence, Deeds, and Signs

"*In the presence....*" Jesus did these signs *in the presence* of the disciples. Another question surfaces here. In the presence of *which disciples*? Is it only to the one who followed him all the way to the cross? What about the ones who followed him until he made what they considered to be a wrong turn? The curious thing here is that Jesus did the signs in the presence of the unbelievers as well as the disciples. *He worked his miracles in public.* To what does this inconsistency point?

Here is the point: these *deeds*, done in the presence of many, were *signs* only to true disciples. The deeds became signs only to those who followed the pointing arrow on the way to finding the Father in Jesus Christ. To others the deeds were simply miracles without meaning. They were events that caused them to wonder. This will become clear as we develop this thought further.

There, but Not There

One key to understanding this distinction between deeds and signs is to notice the implications of the word *presence* as John used it here. Every teacher knows that students can be in class without being *there*. Many students, like Calvin and Hobbs in the old comic strips, are off on some journey into space while the teacher is presenting the material. These students are simply not present to the teaching. They are there in the classroom, but not *there* to the teaching.

During the ministry of Jesus many were on the scene but were not present to the reality of Jesus as the Son of God. They saw the *deeds* but missed the *signs* because they were living in their fantasy world. The only things really *present* to them were the images in their imagination, they were only *present* to the Christ of their fantasy world.

For example, everyone recognized the feeding of the multitude as a supernatural deed, a miracle. They even recognized it as a sign indicating that Jesus was "*the prophet who is coming into the world*" (John 6:14). But when they tried to make him King, Jesus withdrew himself from them. He did not withdraw the natural bread; he withdrew *himself*—the Bread of life. He would not commit himself to the fulfillment of their human expectation. He performed the *deed* in their presence, but the *sign* as he intended it was hidden from them because of their false notions of the coming prophet. They were reading the sign as though it pointed to their fantasy.

The fact that they thought the deed was pointing to the fulfillment of *their* expectation shows that they had not seen the unseen reality of who was there in front of them feeding the multitude. Seeing they did not perceive; hearing they did not understand (Mk. 4:12).

Bread of Life or Bread of Death

When the crowd came for more bread, Jesus tried to draw their attention away from the deed to the sign. "*Do not work for the food which perishes,*" he said, "*but for the food which endures to eternal life, which the Son of Man will give you*" (John 6:27). The arrow of the sign pointed to Jesus himself as the Bread of Life coming down from the Father. He came to gather many "bread-fragments" in "baskets" and take them with him as he returned to his Father. Jesus came to Galilee to give eternal life to all who saw and entered the Way. He said he would raise them up at the last day (John 6:38-39).

To eat of the bread of the *deed*, without following the *sign* to the True Bread, is to partake of what can only sustain a life on its way to death. "*As the living Father sent me, and I live because of the Father,*" Jesus said, "*so he who eats me will live because of me.*" Then he spoke very clearly to those present to the deed but not to the sign. He contrasted the bread in the wilderness with himself as true Bread: "*This is the bread which came down from heaven, not such as the fathers ate and died; he who eats this bread will live forever*" (Jn. 6:57, 58).

The choice is clear. Partake of the bread of the *traditions of your fathers* or partake of the Bread provided by *the Father*. Eat the first and die like your fathers died. Eat the second and live with the Father eternally. Be satisfied with the external blessing of the deed and seek more of that external blessing or follow the sign to find the Father from whom all blessings flow freely and eternally. This looks like a no-brainer to me. Yet many are still satisfied with bread that perishes.

Their choice was determined by their presence or absence to the signs performed before them. "*After this many of his disciples drew back and no longer went about with him*" (John 6:66). The unseen Father was there for them, abiding in the person of Jesus, but their mental bias blinded their minds. They walked away from the Father who was in the Son because they were blind to the pointing of the sign.

Our choice today is determined by our presence or absence to the signs which are written. The same choice is offered in signs he is still performing today for those who have eyes to see. Are you there? Are you present to the signs or only to the wonders? Are you among those who deny that miracles are happening? Where art thou?

Seeing Without Seeing

Like the men of Jeremiah's day, they were "foolish and senseless people, who have eyes, but see not, who have ears, but hear not" (Jer. 5:21). The crowd had seen Jesus in an external way, but they had not seen the Son of the Father because they were satisfied with their human insight. Having eyes, they saw not. They did not see because they did not look for anything deeper than their own human perception.

The Pharisees had heard the voice of Jesus, but they missed the voice of the Father who was speaking (John 5:25). They only listened for statements they could use against him or statements which seemed to confirm their dream-Messiah. Having ears, they did not hear. They did not come out of death into life (John 5:24) because they were content with the life they had, a life on its way to death. That life has no future. That life was on its way to a death that comes from seeing the deed (in an event or in the written text) apart from the Spirit who draws us to the one to whom the sign points.

Paul stated this same truth. He spoke of the Lord who made us competent to be ministers of a new covenant, not in a written text but in the Spirit. He drew attention to the fact that we can read the written text apart from the Spirit and reap the results: "For the written text kills, but the Spirit gives life" (II Cor. 3:6). The written text refers to the biblical text seen by one who does not follow the arrow of the sign to find the one who gives life. The only ones who can follow that arrow are those who are in tune with the Spirit.

Those imprisoned in their dreamworld found fulfillment in their human interpretation of the text. They felt no need to look for anything beyond what they thought they knew. That was a form of bondage worse than a physical prison because they did not know they were in prison. They thought they were free just like the Pharisees who did not acknowledge their bondage (John 8:33).

Reading Scripture Without Listening

Jesus addressed this same problem when he said to the religious leaders, "*You search the scriptures, because you think that in them you have eternal life; and it is they that bear witness to me*" (John 5:39). Even though the Scriptures bear witness to Jesus Christ and his Father there are many who only see doctrines and regulations when they read the text. The Bible is not our Savior; Jesus is. But the Bible does bear witness to him for those who follow the signs of the pointing quill. For others it only points to doctrines and rules.

I still *wake up* sometimes to realize I have been off in my fantasy world again trying to force the text to agree with me. When I go there, I only receive better ideas, not revelation. Looking for the Father in Jesus Christ must follow the line of the pointing finger of the text and receive the miracle of the opened eyes. The power of our cognitive bias is broken by the one to whom the text points, not by the text. We are made free when the Spirit opens our eyes to see him. Are you there? Or are you still in your fantasy?

Let us return to the story of feeding of the multitude. When Jesus turned to the twelve and asked if they would also go away, Peter answered, "*Lord, to whom shall we go? You have the words of eternal life; and we have believed, and have come to know, that you are the Holy One of God*" (John. 6:68-69).

This is an amazing response considering what Jesus had just said: "*Eat my flesh. Drink my blood.*" The disciples did not yet understand the Lord's Supper, the Eucharist, as we know it today. This must have sounded much like a call to cannibalism. Furthermore, the Law forbids the drinking of blood (Lev. 17). How much more repulsive the drinking of human blood must have sounded. Jesus did not try to make their decision easier by explaining what he meant. Nor did he insist they continue to follow. Love does not control.

He left each to make his own decision based on what he or she had already seen and heard. Had they seen the signs or only the deeds? Had they heard the voice of the Father or only the words of *this man* Jesus? Whether they stay or leave will be determined by what they have seen and the level of their believing.

Peter's Example

We can capture the significance of Peter's answer by reading between the lines. Peter was saying, "Lord, we don't understand what you mean about eating your flesh. It sounds like cannibalism, but if that is what it takes to be your disciple, then give me a bite. "Drink my blood" sounds repulsive, and it is against everything we have been taught from the Law. But if the choice is between drinking or going away from you, then fill my cup." The decision to continue following Jesus is always radical.

All the popular ideas and concepts of the Christ were being challenged at their very core. But the twelve (at least for the moment) were willing to leave their concepts behind. If you have really seen him as the Holy One of God, you have no choice but to accept his challenge and leave the ideas in you balloon behind. If you have genuinely believed, you will continue to follow him even if it means turning your back on all you thought you knew. "I am here, and I am staying," is a statement of one who has seen the sign and heard Father's voice.

Present in the Secret Place

Matthew 6:6 will help us understand this concept of being "there but not there". Jesus instructed us to go into our room and close the door when we pray. Then he spoke of the Father being "in secret" and rewarding "in secret."

The secret place is a place where the disciples are present to the Lord and the Lord is present to the disciples. You are in secret and he is in secret. Others may be in the neighborhood, but they are not in this secret place. The closed door to the room is not referring to a literal door. It simply indicates that those who have no relationship with Father have no access to the reality true disciple's experience with Father in this secret place.

Jesus did the *deeds* in public, but the *signs* remained in the secret (*unseen*) place where disciples regularly met? with him and with his Father. Jesus spoke many *words* to the multitude; but Father's *voice* only reached the ears of those willing to forsake their foregone conclusions to follow the Son into and out from the secret place, *Father's bosom*. The disciples saw and heard because they were not merely in the vicinity of Jesus of Nazareth. They were in the presence of the Father who abides in secret, who abides in Jesus and in every true disciple's heart.

They did not fully understand why they were so drawn to Jesus, but they were *there* because the Father was drawing them (John 6:44). They were in that secret place because of their willingness to continue following Jesus even when his way surprised them and challenged their preconceived notions.

Even though Peter did not follow Jesus all the way to the place of his crucifixion, he did follow Jesus. He stumbled as he followed, but he followed. Like the other disciples, his understanding of the way Jesus was going was clouded. But when Jesus made a turn which Peter had not anticipated; Peter continued to follow at a distance. He did have preconceived notions, but he forsook them to follow Jesus the way Jesus was going. He did deny the Lord in a moment of confusion, but he was the first to enter the empty tomb. He was still following despite his failure to understand.

Are you in that place where Peter was? Are you ready to be surprised and challenged by Jesus? Are you ready to follow him to the bosom of the Father?

Chapter Five
Transition from the Old to the New

So far, we have noticed the danger of coming to the Scriptures with preconceived notions. We also noticed that the mental pictures in our imagination influence what we see. These embedded notions may keep us from seeing what is right in front of us. John wrote his Gospel using the stories as signs to challenge the images in our balloon. He wanted us to see the relationship between the Father and the Son as we follow the story line. He wanted us to see the Father's love and become believing disciples, disciples who are present to the Father who is in Jesus. He knew that in believing we would receive life in him.

Our next project will be to look at the prologue and the four consecutive days in the first chapter of John's Gospel. As we unpack these verses, we will be looking for signs of the transition from the Old Testament to Jesus Christ and the Church. We will begin by looking briefly at the poetic structure of the first chapter of John. John hinted at the meaning of the signs by the structure he imposed on the stories he told in his Gospel. Again, the structure is not the point, *the structure points to the point.*

The Structure of John's First Chapter

The prologue (John. 1:1-18) presents the basic structure of the relation between God, his Word, and his world. The structure is divided into seven sections. The center of the poetic structure of the text speaks of God giving "*power to become children of God*" to those who believe and receive the Word (vs.12-13). The ability to become children of God is the central theme of the prologue and the central point of the whole Gospel. Before and after that center John develops three other themes. Before the center (vs. 1-11) the focus is on God's relationship to the world in general as he moves toward the sending of his Son in the flesh. After the center (vs. 14-18) the focus is on the coming of the Son and his ministry to those who receive him, who have become sons and daughters of God.

This text is structured like a menorah. The central "candle" is the main point and lights up the meaning of those verses before and those after the center.

On either side of that center there is mention of this Word which is the light of man coming into the world. Immediately before the center (9-11) the Word came as light to those who were his own, but they reject that light. Immediately after the center the Word comes in the flesh and the disciples who received him (the "we" of verse 14) beheld his glory. That is the first theme on either side of the center—the coming of the Word into the world he created, rejected by some, and received by others.

As we move another step away from the center, we find John the Baptist and his testimony. Before the center it is a negative testimony. "*He was not the light but came to bear witness to the light*" (6-8). As we move forward another step from the center, it is the Baptist's positive testimony. "*He who comes after me is before me*" (15). That is the second theme—the negative and positive testimony of John.

One more step back from the center, the prologue begins with the relation of God to the Word, "*...the Word was with God, and the Word was God*" (vs.1-5). This Word was active in creating and giving life and light to mankind. One more step forward from the center, the prologue ends with the Word of God identified as the "*only Son, who is in the bosom of the Father*" (vs. 16-18). It is this Son that makes the Father known to those who believe in him. That is the third theme—the relationship of *God to his Word* in creation on the one side, and on the other side the relation of the *Father to the Son* and the Son's ministry to the world he created. That Son is *this man*, Jesus.

The *sign* of this *structure* points to God's dealings with the man he created and man's response to his coming. Mankind--his own--first rejected his presence among them, but he overcame that rejection by becoming part of his creation through what we call the incarnation. In this way he accomplished a *new creation*, a family of sons and daughters. The central point of the prologue is that those who receive the Son become sons and daughters of his Father.

We should not only think of the 'before and after' as referring to chronological time before and after Christ. It can also refer to the condition of individuals in the world before and after they "*see the light*" and receive Christ. Before their eyes are opened, Jesus is among them as one they do not know. The "old man" becomes a "new man" when he sees the light of the glory of God in the face of Jesus Christ (II Cor. 4:6). In John, that experience is called being "born from above" (John. 3:7).

As we present the following meditations, be alert to John's presentation of the transition from the ministry of the Baptist to the ministry of Jesus. That theme is presented in a series of four days.

The transition follows a pattern like what we noticed above in the prologue but with a different structure. The Baptist's negative testimony (first day) was followed by the Baptist's positive testimony (second day). The transition began as two of the Baptist's disciples heard his second positive testimony and began to follow Jesus (third day). Jesus then began the process of calling disciples to himself and the Baptist was left behind (fourth day). The transition was complete.

Four Days of Transition

So, after the prologue John presented the transition from John the Baptist (the old creation) to Jesus (the new creation) over four consecutive days (John. 1:19-51). In this chapter we will focus on the third day when two disciples heard John's testimony and followed Jesus. These two disciples become a sign pointing to the kind of following that leaves the old behind and turns to partake of the new. They point to the way to enter the reality of what the Father offers in Jesus Christ the Son. These two disciples will hold our attention all the way through the rest of this volume because they really heard and really followed Jesus to the place prepared for them—the abiding place in Father's bosom.

First, before we focus on the third day, we will present a brief overview of the other days to set the stage. After each overview we will state the meaning of the "sign" of that day.

Overview: First Day

On the *first* day Jewish leaders sent priests and Levites from Jerusalem to check out the Baptist. They were trying to find out if he was claiming to be Messiah (John. 1:19-28).

"*I am not the Christ,*" John confessed. His answer was short. God did not send him to testify about himself. So, he said no more until they press him.

"*Are you Elijah?*" the inquisitors asked.

"*I am not.*" His answer was briefer still.

"*Are you the prophet?*" They needed an answer for those who had sent them.

"*No,*" he replied.

Why was John being so short with these men? He was sent to bear witness to Jesus, the coming Messiah, so why was he avoiding the issue? I will tell you. Because he knew that those who sent these men were not truly seeking Messiah. They came to judge the Baptist. This happened near Bethany, which means *House of Sorrow*.

John often used places and times to alert the reader to the spiritual realities the sign was pointing to. Here is the message of Bethany: "How sad it is when we are in that place where heaven's messenger withholds his testimony."

Here is the point of the first day: "*Heaven withholds its testimony from those who set themselves up as judges of religious orthodoxy.*"

Overview: Second Day

On the *second* day (John 1:29-34), John gave a positive testimony. Pointing to Jesus, he said, "*Behold, the Lamb of God, who takes away the sin of the world.*" Seeing the Holy Spirit descend on Jesus as a dove, he proclaimed: "*This is the Son of God.*" He delivered this testimony as Jesus was walking toward him on this second day. John could not have spoken more clearly, "God sent me to point out *this man* Jesus. He is the one God promised would come; he is more than you expected. He is not just another man; he is the Lamb of God; the Spirit of God is upon him. He is the Son of God."

There is no record of anyone turning to follow on the second day. John may have left out that detail to draw attention to the sign. Many may have chased after him on that second day thinking he was the fulfillment of their expectations. Chasing after God is not the same as chasing the image in your mind's eye. Chasing after God is turning to follow when you have really heard the testimony of his messenger. That may be why many chase God and never find him. They are only chasing their dream. By God's grace the blessings and promises are still available even to those who do not get it yet.

Here is the message of the second day: "*God fulfills all his promises in this man Jesus. We receive the removal of sin and power for living life by the Spirit through him.*" (Later we will discuss a distinction between the removal of sin and forgiveness.)

We will save the third day for later. Since it is the main point of this chapter it will require more attention.

Overview: Fourth Day

On the *fourth* day (John 1:43-51) Jesus began to call his own disciples and his disciples began to call others. The Baptist was no longer active. Andrew found Philip and Philip found Nathaniel. Jesus' disciples invited others to *come and see*.

The transition is now complete. At the end of this fourth day Jesus recognized Nathaniel and affirmed him as "*an Israelite with no guile.*" The phrase *without guile* points to one whose *balloon* is already deflated and ready to receive revelation. Nathaniel immediately confessed, "*Rabbi, you are the Son of God! You are the king of Israel!*" Jesus promised Nathaniel, "*You will see heaven opened, and the angels of God ascending and descending upon the Son of Man.*" This image reflects the story of Jacob at Bethel, the House of God, where angels ascended and descended (Gen. 29:10-17).

The Baptist had identified Jesus as the Son of God on the second day. After Nathaniel's confession on the fourth day, however,

Jesus used the term *Son of Man*. This term carries some baggage from Jewish apocalyptic expectations developed between the close of the Old testament and the coming of Jesus into the world. It also carries baggage from the Persian Zarathustra (an Iranian prophet contemporary with Moses). The Son of Man in Jewish apocalyptic writing was somewhat influenced by that Persian image. Friedrich Nietzsche (died 1900 AD) used Zarathustra's image of the Son of Man to introduce his concept of the *Superman* (Uber Mann) who allegedly took over after the supposed *Death of God*. (That was the final shift into modern humanism.)

In Ezekiel, however, the term simply means *human being* or *son of Adam*. Taking our lead from Ezekiel, we suggest that the angels ascending and descending on the Son of Man may refer to the work of angels on behalf of all those sons of Adam (that includes us) who join Jesus in his resurrection appearances and enter the "*New Testament Bethel*", which is Body of Christ, the *one new man* (Eph. 2:15). The angels ascending and descending which Nathanael would see were angels ministering to those who are being saved (Heb. 1:13). Jesus was Son of Man (he was human) and the Son of God. We are his brothers and sisters; *we are the many sons and daughters brought to glory* (Heb. 2:10). We are the one New Man of Ephesians 2:15.

Here is the message of the fourth day: "*Those with an open heart (balloon without guile) will see heaven opened and will have angels serving them as they become actively involved in the coming of the Kingdom.*"

The Third Day in Scripture

In Scripture, the *third* day often marks the conclusion of a spiritual journey which begins a new journey at the same time. The beginning of something new requires that the old to be left behind. On a *third* day Abraham lifted his eyes and beheld the place where he would offer Isaac as a sacrifice. On that *third* day Abraham and Isaac became something they were not before, a picture (a type) of the Father offering his Son (Gen. 22:4). On a *third* day the Lord appeared on Mount Sinai to meet with his people (Ex. 19). On a *third* day, God *"will raise us up that we may live before him"* (Hos. 6:2). Being raised up is clearly the beginning of a new life in the presence of God.

There are many other examples: Joseph released his brothers from prison, Jonah was rescued from the belly of the whale, Esther fasted before entering the king's presence to plead for the life of the Jewish people, Jesus was raised from the grave—all these were third day events.

In the final chapter of John, Jesus' third appearance (not a third day, but still significant) was after he ascended to his Father and returned to bring the disciples into the place he had gone to prepare for them (John 14:2). This event also speaks of a new thing in the lives of the disciples who had believed in Jesus and made themselves available for the advancement of his kingdom.

The Wedding in Cana follows this transition from John to Jesus. That event also takes place on a *third* day (John 2:1). The point of the wedding feast is that Jesus *"manifested his glory; and his disci-*

ples believed in him" (John 2:11). We will discover that Jesus' glory is related to his abiding in the bosom of the Father. That will have to wait for volume two.

Here is the message of the third day in John chapter one: *"We are invited to leave our present place and enter a new abiding place with Jesus, that place where God's glory is revealed to us and through us to others."*

Standing and Walking on the Third Day

Let us look at this *third* day more closely. *"The next day again John was standing with two of his disciples; and he looked at Jesus as he walked, and said, 'Behold the Lamb of God!' The two disciples heard him say this, and they followed Jesus"* (John 1:35-37).

"John was standing." On this third day the Baptist, who had been on the move, was now standing and Jesus, who had been standing, was walking. *That is a sign.* It points to a shift, a radical transition that was about to occur. Everything up to this point was preparing the way for Jesus' public ministry. From this point forward all the stories and dialogues were designed to offer the reader an intimate relationship with Father through Jesus who is the Word of the (*unseen*) Father in flesh.

On the *first day,* John was the central figure and Jesus was not even mentioned by name. Jesus was *standing* in the crowd as *"one whom you do not know."* On the *second day,* John saw Jesus *"coming toward him."* Jesus was beginning to move, but John was still the actor of that day. On that that third day, John was standing and no longer moving; Jesus was *walking*. John was decreasing; Jesus was increasing (John 3:30).

The Big Shift

This sign does not merely point to a shift in the story; it points to a shift in world history. Before this, everything is moving toward Jesus Christ. The Law and the prophets, including the Baptist, bear witness to his *coming*. After that, the Apostles with the Church bear witness that *he has come in the flesh*. Through him all things will be reconciled to the Father (Col. 1:20). The final goal of creation is now in view.

This third day marks the passing of the old and the coming of the new. In the culmination of the coming Kingdom, God will make all things new (Rev. 21:5). This third day was a pivotal point in history. The ministry of the Baptist, and with him all the Old Testament prophets, found his true goal on this third day. It was the conclusion of the old way. Something ended for good. Something new began for better.

This third day marks the end of a remarkably long Night through Old Testament times. It also marks the beginning of a New Day. The light has begun to dawn, for the glory of the Lord has risen (Isa. 60:1). The sign of this day points to the day of his resurrection when Jesus makes his Father available to the world in a new way. In other words, this third day points to the *ministry* of the resurrected Jesus. But the *events* of this day also point to the place Jesus prepared for us to live in the Father's love.

From that place in Father's bosom Jesus will send the Church into the world to draw others into the peaceful life of the Father, Son and Holy Spirit. All the events in this Gospel happen as Jesus was making his way towards the cross to prepare a place for mankind in Father's loving embrace. All these events point as signs to the way we come into Father's bosom and go out from that abiding place into the world with God's love.

John's Disciples

"*...with two of his disciples.*" A group of men had gathered around the Baptist. He had disciples. An excitement hovered over Israel in those days because they were expecting Messiah to make his appearance soon. They expected a king to appear and re-establish the throne of David in Jerusalem, leading them into victory over the Roman invaders. The Baptist was not the one they were looking for (he was not the light). He came to bear witness to the one who would come after him, who ranked before him.

The transition from the Baptist to Jesus was not obvious at that time—not even to John and his disciples. Most of them remained with him. Even John struggled with the ministry of Jesus later. Luke told of John sending two of his disciples to ask Jesus, "*Are you the one who is to come, or shall we look for another?*" (Lk. 7:19). Nevertheless, in the moment of revelation on this second day of our text the Baptist was not struggling. He clearly and boldly identified Jesus as the Son of God. It is interesting that his testimony was more complete on the second day than on this third day.

The Eye of a Prophet

"He looked at Jesus." John was looking at the external features of the one who was walking toward him. He was looking with the eye of a prophet, an eye that is always open and ready for God to show something beyond the surface, something unseen by the natural eye. He was considering the spiritual implications of what his eyes were beholding. He had not been sent to bear witness to what he might be able to discover with his natural human insight. He knew human insight would not help him recognize the one he had been sent to identify.

"I myself did not know him," he declared the day before, indicating his own inability to see without help from above (John 1:33). As he looked at Jesus on this third day, he was waiting for God to show him more of the unseen reality he was looking at.

This raises a question: Why is he looking so intently on this third day? On the previous day he had seen Jesus coming toward him. He had seen the Holy Spirit descend upon him and remain. God had told him earlier that the one on whom he saw the Holy Spirit descend and remain would be the one he should identify to the people. If he had already seen so clearly, why was he so eager to see again? The answer is simple. He was not satisfied with having seen yesterday. He wanted to see more clearly today.

He understood the principle implied in the statement, *"His mercies...are new every morning"* (Lam. 3:22-23). Each day holds a promise of entering more deeply into the mystery of God's presence among us, a more profound experience of what we saw and heard yesterday. The reality does not change but our experience of it and our ability to communicate what we have seen and heard does increase. The Baptist was waiting for the more God had for him.

We must never be satisfied with having received yesterday. What he has for us today is new. Yesterday's manna breeds worms (Ex. 16:20) but God gives fresh provision daily. To receive the newness, we must be open for him to show it to us again today in a new way. We must strive to see more deeply today than we saw yesterday. We must not take what we saw yesterday and hold it so tightly that we become unable to see more clearly today. It is far too easy to stuff a new image into our balloon based on our interpretation of what he showed us yesterday.

None of us has seen perfectly and none of us has seen it all. God may have something new to add to our understanding today. We are all in process and must remain open to new insights. Life in Christ is a journey with a destination beyond what any of us have understood or received so far. We can walk that way only by faith, by being in the grasp of the one who has apprehended us.

Making the Father Known by Walking

"...*as he walked*." The Baptist gave his testimony on this third day based on the way Jesus walked. John was not merely telling us that Jesus happened to be on foot that day. By the time he wrote his Gospel he had been meditating on the events of the life of Jesus for over fifty years. He had seen much more—and more deeply—in his later years than what he had seen in his early experiences with Jesus. He wrote his "book of signs" to help us see the *more* he had seen and experienced.

This *more* can be seen through the grid of the death, burial, and resurrection of Jesus and the subsequent outpouring of the Holy Spirit. If it took John over fifty years of seeking for new insights before he was ready to write about what he saw, we should not be surprised or feel guilty if it takes us more than one reading before we begin to see what he saw.

Jesus revealed the Father by the *way he walked*. This is one of John's major themes. His walk—the way he lived life—was a sign pointing to the Father. "*No one has ever seen God,*" John wrote. We cannot know God except by revelation, and Jesus was that revelation: "*The only Son, who is in the bosom of the Father, he has made him known*" (John 1:18). The Greek translated "made known" implies making known in narrative form. Jesus made the Father known by narrative of his life, by the way he walked.

John used the present tense to indicate that the bosom of the Father is the *eternal abiding place* of the Son. When this eternal Word became flesh, he did not cease to be the Son of God nor did he leave his Father's bosom. When Jesus repeatedly said, "*I am in the Father,*" he was referring to his eternal abiding place in his Father's loving embrace. He came out from his Father's bosom without leaving the Father's bosom. He occupied that place even while on the earth. From that place in Father's bosom he made the Father known. His purpose in coming was to return to the Father bringing "*many sons to glory*" (Heb. 2:10).

In the next chapter we will attempt to bring more clarity to the concept of the bosom of the Father. Like all other concepts, this one is capable of being misunderstood and misrepresented.

Chapter Six

The Bosom of the Father

Look closely at John 1:18 for two insights, "*The only Son, who is in the bosom of the Father, he has made him known.*" First, the Greek word *kolpos*, translated "bosom," refers to that part of the body that is in front between the arms. According to Thayer's lexicon it can also refer to that fold of the loose clothing above the girdle that was used to safely carry valuables -something like a fanny pack, but in the front. Jesus lived his life in his Father's "tummy pack." Wherever the Father went, the Son went with him because he was abiding in the tummy pack.

With this image we can speak of a place in God which protects and nourishes the new life of those who, having been born of God, find their place there. Jesus, abiding in the Father's bosom, was himself that place from which the New Creation was destined to emerge as many would come to believe in his name and allow themselves to be brought into the Father's eternal embrace.

When you see Jesus, if you really see what is in front of you, you are looking at his Father. If you are in Christ, you are in his Father's tummy pack, in his protective custody. If you are in him, you are also going where he is going because your new life is *hidden with Christ in God* (Col. 3:3). This is what John had in mind when he spoke of the beloved disciple reclining on Jesus' breast (John 13:23). The word translated *breast* is *kolpos*, the same word translated *bosom* in 1:18. All disciples are welcome in that position of intimacy, but none are forced to recline there. Love does not control.

The full implication of this image of the bosom is much deeper than the tummy pack. The tummy pack is still external to the Father. Everyone desires to have a place in someone's heart. The message of the bosom speaks of being in the Father's heart of love. Jesus went to prepare a place in Father's heart for all who come to the Son. St. Augustine was right when he said we are all restless until we find that place. When we do find it, we have found the treasure in a field and will be willing to sell everything to have that treasure for ourselves.

When I first received this insight, I used the metaphor of the Father's lap. We are invited into the Father's lap of love. That is a good picture of intimacy, but for our purpose the tummy pack is better. A person's lap is not available unless he is in a sitting position. The Father is indeed seated on the throne, but he is also highly active in the history of the world. He is moving in the earth while he sits on his throne. We need to rid ourselves of our either-or thinking.

I prefer the image of the tummy pack over the lap for reasons beyond the fact that the lap disappears when the person rises from his sitting position. The image of Father's lap can lead to a static concept, like sitting in the lap of the statue of an important person. Neither the statue nor the one sitting is moving. A static image is an

The Bosom of the Father

idol. For that reason, I prefer the more dynamic image of the tummy pack of one who is on the move. Our God is always on the move and he carries us with him if we are willing to go along for the ride.

So, I use the tummy pack image to emphasize God's movement into the world with those who abide in him. Here we distinguish between our position and our walk. We are in him. That is our *position*. But there is more, *we are in what he is doing as well; and he is in what we are doing* as we obey his voice. To abide in Christ (*our position*) means we are moved when he moves. We are in him and he is in us. If we are active in doing his will on earth as it is in heaven, then for him to be in us means he is moving when we move. So, he is *in our doing* (*our walk*) as we do what we see him doing in the earth today. That is our *walk*.

What we are trying to capture here is a dynamic image of our *being carried along with him in what he is doing*. He is moving toward the consummation of all things—toward the uniting of all things in Jesus Christ, things in heaven and things in earth (Eph. 1:10). As he moves forward, we are in his tummy pack—in his heart—and we are involved in his willing and doing in the earth. We experience the intimacy of Father's bosom as we join him in his work of loving the world.

Henri Nouwen, in his book *The Return of the Prodigal Son*, spoke of "the One who awaits me with open arms and wants to hold me in an eternal embrace." While working with mentally handicapped people, Nouwen experienced enough of the Father's embrace to make him hungry for more. We are saying that those of us who abide in Christ are already in that eternal embrace even while we go with longing toward a deeper experience of that embrace. It is from that embrace that we should be reaching out to embrace our neighbor. When we reach out to others, we will experience a deeper sense of his love for us as well.

Teaching by Life Narrative

The second insight is related to the word which is translated "*made him known.*" That word can refer to a Rabbi presenting a narrative, a story to illustrate a teaching (Thayer). That is what Jesus was doing when he told parables. But the life Jesus lived on earth in the bosom of the Father became *a living narrative*, a *living parable*, a life which revealed the character of the Father as it unfolded on his way to the cross and out from the cross to Pentecost and into the church. John presented a written narrative of Jesus' life because he wanted us to find that abiding place in Father's bosom. From that position we are representatives of the Father as he manifests his Love to the world through us.

As we read this narrative of Jesus' life, our life can become a narrative that unfolds the character of the Father through us as well. "*He who says he abides in him ought to walk in the same way in which he walked*" (I John 2:6). John's written narratives of Jesus' life and teachings show us how Jesus walked, how he lived his life out from his abiding relationship with his Father. We are invited to follow him into that abiding relationship and live our life on earth out from that place in him. When we walk in the same way he walked *our life becomes an episode in the ongoing narrative of his life lived in his Body today.*

The Walk and the Abiding Place

John wants us to connect Jesus' *walk* with his being in that *abiding place* in the Father's bosom. His abiding in the Father makes his walk a revelation of Father's love for the world. Later Jesus would tell Philip, "*He who has seen me has seen the Father*" (John 14:9). Everything Jesus said and did was a revelation of Father's love because the works he did were not his works. "*...the Father who dwells in me is doing his works*" (John 14:10). A call to follow *this man* is an invitation to dwell in his Father's acts of love for our neighbors, our community, and our nation.

Jesus was not the source of his own life; "*For as the Father has life in himself, so he has granted the Son also to have life in himself*" (John 5:26). Out of the life of the Father came the living and doing of the Son; "*the son can do nothing of his own accord, but only what he sees the Father doing*" (John 5:19). The Son initiated nothing. He followed his Father in all things. From that place of abiding in the Father, his walk revealed his Father to those who had eyes to see. That was how he walked, and the Baptist saw the *Lamb of God* in that walk. We are invited to walk as he walked and become sons and daughters who make the Father known by the way we walk.

The Baptist could not have fully understood the significance of Jesus' walk at that early stage. Paul's phrase, he saw "in a mirror darkly" (I Cor. 13:12), is appropriate here. Even the closest disciples did not understand these events until after the resurrection. Our point here is that this way of referring to Jesus "as he walked" is evidence of the way John used stories as signs pointing beyond themselves. This Jewish literary device (called *Midrash*) was his way of tempting the reader to look at the text more closely.

The more I study John's Gospel, the more I am convinced that John, the beloved disciple, was planting seeds in passages to prepare us for a deeper revelation of the death and resurrection when his unfolding narrative brings us to that point at the end of his Gospel. As we follow the many pointing arrows within this Gospel, we will always find the glory of God the Father in the life, death, and resurrection of Jesus the Son. Once we understand this, we can even see the cross in the way he walked.

What Did John See?

"*Behold, the Lamb of God.*" As we noticed, the testimony of the third day is shorter than the second day's testimony. The second day highlighted what he will do for you. He will take away your sins. He will empower you to live in the kingdom of God by baptizing you in the Holy Spirit. You will be able to heal the sick, cast out demons, and raise the dead. He will give you a new past. You will no longer be what you were. You will be sons and daughters of the living God. And he will give you a new future in the bosom of his Father. You will live in him and be able to live your life here and now through him.

If all these blessings are reflected in the testimony of the second day, what makes the third day more significant? Here is the answer.

The testimony of the third day—*Behold, the Lamb of God*—focuses on *who he is*. There was no mention of what he will do for you.

The Lord is not looking for followers who are obsessed with what he will do for them. He does not want disciples who merely desire to work miracles or to receive miracles. He is looking for those who recognize him for who he *is* and follow him even if this following gets them into trouble. He certainly promised blessings and he is faithful to bestow blessings, but those who crave blessings can never follow as true disciples.

The multitudes chased after the blessings—bread, healing, hope of political dominance, etc. If the blessings were forthcoming, they continued to follow; but when he offered what he really had for them, they drew back and no longer went about with him (John 6:66). The point: *Those who seek him for who he really IS will continue with him even when his way goes contrary to their expectations.*

Passover and Atonement

To understand the significance of the third day, we must pay attention to phrase *"Lamb of God."* In the testimony of the second day John added the phrase *"who takes away the Sin of the world."* Although there are many sacrifices involving lambs, we generally understand Jesus as the true Passover Lamb sacrificed on the cross during that Passover Feast. In the book of Revelation, we see the Lion of Judah which turns out to be the Lamb that was slain (Rev. 5:5-6).

Jesus is the Lamb that was slain, and he did take away our Sin, but that is not a concept related to Passover. We mentioned earlier that forgiveness is different from taking away Sin. We will now explain the significance of that distinction. There is more to John's testimony than Jesus being the Passover Lamb. Understanding exactly what John meant by combining the "Lamb of God" with the "taking away Sin" will help us uncover the deeper implications of the sign of the third day. There is a marvelous mystery in this combination. (We will explain the capitol "S" below)

Passover: Deliverance and Covenant Fellowship

The Passover feast commemorated deliverance from Egyptian bondage and the protection of the first-born of Israel from death, but it was never related to taking away Sin. The taking away of Sin is not even mentioned in the Exodus narrative of Passover. So why does the Baptist mention taking Sin away in connection with the Lamb (Jesus) who will be slaughtered during this Passover Feast?

The Passover lamb was not burnt on the altar as a sin offering; it was eaten as a sign of being partners in the altar (I Cor. 10:18). The phrase, *partners in the altar*, simply means that the one who eats of the sacrificial animal acknowledges and experiences covenant fellowship with the God to whom the altar is dedicated. So, the Passover Lamb reminded worshipers that they had been delivered from bondage and that they were in a covenant relationship with the God who rescued them.

Atonement: Forgiveness and Taking Away Sin

The Passover lamb offered in the Spring Festival did not symbolize the removal of Sin. Dealing with Sin was the work of *two other animals* selected for the Day of Atonement in the fall festival. One animal represented *forgiveness* and atonement—a sin offering. The priests burned its carcass on the altar and the High Priest took its blood into the Holy of Holies and sprinkled it on the lid of the Ark of the Covenant. It is interesting that the sins of the people were not pronounced over this animal before it was slaughtered.

The second animal represented the *taking away of* Sin. The Sin of the people was symbolically transferred to the scapegoat by the laying on of hands. Then it was taken outside the camp with the national Sin on its head and released in the wilderness (Lev. 6). Sin was thus taken "outside the camp."

The historical transition from the Old Testament types to the reality of fulfillment happened in three days—the days of Jesus' death, burial, and resurrection. So, the sign of the third day of our text points to this transition from type to fulfillment, from the picture of liberation to the reality of freedom from bondage to Sin and entrance into intimacy with God. This Christ Event was the transition from the old to the new creation. History passed from the shadow of a person to real presence of *this man*.

So, we see two separate feasts with three different animals, all rich with meaning. Was John confused in his terminology? I think not. John intentionally combined the meaning of the two feasts into one. He had seen Jesus Christ as the fulfillment of both feasts. In fact, when he mentioned the baptism of the Holy Spirit earlier, he included the Feast of Pentecost as well. Jesus is the reality that all the sacrifices and rituals of the old covenant refer to, not just Passover.

John's connecting of the Passover and the Day of Atonement recognized that the bondage in Egypt was not a result of the sins of the people. Passover memorialized the deliverance from that bondage. But the people had been in Babylonian captivity because of their continued idolatry and rebellion against the word of God through the prophets. Their bondage to Rome was simply a continuation of their bondage due to Sin. It was necessary to include the two Feasts together because freedom from Sin and deliverance from bondage were the same thing. That Sin must be taken away, outside the camp, to accomplish eternal redemption. (A. T. Wright, *The Day the Revolution Began* is helpful here.)

Guilt and Tendency

Our sins are forgiven, *and Sin is* taken away in and through Jesus Christ. Forgiveness deals with guilt—and forgiveness is a good thing. But we should never be satisfied with forgiveness alone. We should desire for him to take the *tendency* to sin out of our midst—outside the camp. The blood of bulls and goats was never able to *take away* the tendency to sin (Heb. 10:4-11). God forgave sinful deeds in the Old Testament. David knew forgiveness personally and spoke a blessing over those whose sins are forgiven (Ps. 32:1). Forgiveness was always available because Father God always loved the world he created.

The primary act of love in a fallen world is forgiveness, and that forgiveness has always been available in God for those who turn to him. However, the *tendency to sin* was not *taken away*. The fullness of time had not yet come. The "*real*" blood of atonement had not yet been shed. The real Goat had not been deserted, separated from the people of God, and abandoned "outside the gate."

Taking away the *tendency to sin* adds a new dimension to forgiveness. We have often missed the significance of this dimension of the work of Christ on the cross. It seems to me that in these last days God desires to bring the Church into a revelation of this dimension and give us the full experience of this removal of Sin.

Those Old Testament sacrifices were signs, symbols, or types of a reality available through the shed blood of Jesus. The Old Testament saints repeated these sacrifices year after year because they had not received the reality of the cleansed conscience (Heb. 10:2-3). The sacrifices of the Day of Atonement were only a shadow of the reality that took place at the cross. What is that reality?

A Cleansed Conscience

Our hearts are "*sprinkled clean from an evil conscience*" when the blood of *this man* is applied (Heb. 10:22). Life activities flow from the heart (Prov. 4:23). The heart and conscience work together in determining our action. The conscience is more than the good or bad feelings when we have done something. Conscience refers to the source of our behavior, not an inner voice trying to make us feel good or bad because of our behavior. Our conscience is the dynamic within us that presses us to act in a certain way depending on the situation we face. *An evil conscience produces evil activity. A clean conscience produces clean activity.* This is the power of Sin.

The cleansing of the conscience *takes away* that *inclination* to sin that we struggle with so desperately. It takes away the evil inclination of the imagination of our heart (Gen. 6:5). It liberates us from the dominion of Sin (Rom. 6:14). We are no longer slaves to Sin (Rom. 6:16). Sin with a capitol "S" refers to the power of Sin to enslave us, to bring us under its authority as a slave. That power to enslave operates through the conscience, through the "imaginations of the heart" (Gen. 6:5) which tempted Eve, which invited the flood, and continues to enslave mankind even in our day.

John made a radical statement in his first letter. "*You know that he appeared to take away sins, and in him there is no Sin. No one who abides in him sins; no one who sins has either seen him or known him*" (I John 3:5-6). John tied the idea of taking away sins to a life of victory over Sin. To the degree that we abide in him—in the way John's Gospel used the term abide—to that degree we will not sin because the tendency is gone.

Someone may ask, "Why then do we still have the tendency to sin if it has been taken away?" The answer is simple. All God's blessings are received by faith. The sins of the whole world are covered by the work of Jesus on the cross (II Cor. 5:19), but that work has its effect only in the life of those who believe and receive. What would happen if a generation truly received this "cleansed conscience" by faith? *Imagine a generation whose conscience is purified from dead works to serve the living God* (Heb. 9:14)? What a Day that would be! That Day is the kingdom of God in the earth. Deliverance from the tendency to sin is coming as believing increases in the land.

If we continue to *believe* that we are bound, we will continue to be in bondage to Sin. The transition is complete as far as the work of Jesus Christ is concerned; "it is finished." But the church is still on the way to receiving the full experience of what is available in Christ. We are not yet a spotless Bride, but we will be. Remember that biblical believing is not about a doctrine, it is about being grasped and held by the one who has redeemed us from the *futile ways inherited from our fathers* (I Pet. 3:18). When that truth grabs you, it will take you into the reality of liberation from Sin. Join me on the way to that.

Each generation is challenged to go farther on this path than the previous generation. We are going toward that time when "*the creation itself will be set free from its bondage to decay and obtain the glorious liberty of the children of God*" (Rom. 8:21). In fact, "*the whole creation has been groaning in travail together until now,*" waiting for the "*revealing of the sons of God*" (Rom. 8:19, 22). Someday God will show his sons to be revealed as what they really are because they will really believe the gospel and be made free from Sin.

Active Waiting in Full Fellowship

We are now waiting for "*adoption as sons, the redemption of our bodies*" (Rom. 8:23). We should be actively waiting, by striving to enter that rest (Heb. 4:11) where we no longer struggle with unbelief and deeds of darkness, where our conscience is cleansed. Each of us must do our part in this generation to prepare the way for the next generation to go a step farther. Do you dare believe that the Lamb of God made available the removal of your tendency to sin? Will you choose to walk toward real freedom from Sin?

Summary of Passover and Atonement

In summary, Jesus is the true Passover Lamb of God who delivers us from the world system and brings us into a covenant relationship with his Father. The covenant is established, and we may regularly partake of the covenant meal. In the Lord's Supper we are not partaking of a dead lamb. He is alive. Dare to *believe into that*. He is also the Atonement sacrifice and the Scapegoat. He has reconciled us to God and taken Sin outside the camp.

As we abide in him, we move toward possessing our inheritance in the "land of promise." If we remain in his *tummy pack*, we will continue to have victory over our enemies (including Sin). Father has provided the way if we would only walk in it. Jesus is the way out of the bondage to Sin into the Father's bosom where *victory over sin tendencies is the norm*. He provided a way for our evil inclination to be taken away and our evil conscience to be cleansed. Are you receiving that? Are you believing into that?

Leaving Sin Behind

If we see Jesus *as he walked,* we find the Father making his grace and truth available to the world. All the animals slaughtered through the centuries were only types and shadows of this Lamb who is, even now (in this Gospel narrative), being led to his death on the cross during the Passover Feast. On that wooden altar he will become a sin offering, fulfilling the Day of Atonement. He will take Sin with him outside the camp into the grave thus removing the obstacle to reconciliation with the Father and fulfilling the image of the Scapegoat. In that act he also promises deliverance from the bondage to the *old world* of violence (Sin) for those who apply the blood of the covenant to the "door posts" of their lives and cross over to the *new world* of Love in Christ.

From that grave his Father will raise him up on the third day, leaving Sin behind. (All our "junk" is in the grave if we genuinely believe in his name.) Jesus will then make himself available by the Holy Spirit as we follow him into Father's bosom. Through his resurrection we become partners with him who was dead and is now alive forevermore (Rev. 1:18). Through his flesh and blood, we are brought into the community of fellowship in the Father's bosom. *We are flesh and blood sons and daughters of God.* That is what it means to eat his flesh and drink his blood.

Jesus accomplished more than a geographical removal of Sin to a place outside the city gate of Jerusalem. The scapegoat points to a reality that is in Jesus Christ. Sin is really left outside the camp for us when we live in the Father's loving embrace. Sin no longer has dominion over us (Rom. 6:14).

To the degree that we abide in the Father's bosom—his tummy pack, his heart—to that degree we overcome Sin. We can still hold on to our sins if we choose, but why? Have we attached ourselves to something outside the Father's heart of love? Why would we want to do that? Do we dare believe this freedom is available for us?

Believing is entering the *path* to total freedom. Being on the path is not the same as arriving at the destination. Abiding in his word is continuing to walk on the path as a disciple. It is only as we continue walking on the path that we come to know the truth and are made freer each day (John. 8:31-32). How far do we want to go on this path? Are we satisfied with simply being on the path or do we want to go all the way?

Making the Father Known

Jesus walked in a way that revealed the Father's heart of love by doing "*only what he saw the Father doing.*" Living his life in this way, Jesus revealed an important truth: The Father is for us; he is not against us. Jesus is not trying to protect us from an angry God. He is not trying to *change* God's heart toward man. He is *revealing* the true heart of the Father to man. The desire of the Father has always been to have intimate fellowship with his creation. "*For God so loved the world that he gave his only begotten Son*" (John. 3:16). That is the Father of love. That is what Jesus came to show us about his Father. His Father loves us and is available to become effective as our Father.

God the Father Seeking Man

The Bible is not a story of man seeking God. It is a story of God seeking man (see Abraham Heschel's, *God in Search of Man*). After Adam sinned in the garden, he did not seek God or try to placate him and make amends. Adam covered himself with fig leaves, hid from God, and blamed Eve.

Like the Prodigal son, man is always running from the Father into a far country and blaming God for his predicament. Or, like the Elder brother, man keeps on working in the religious field trying to earn what is already his and resenting God for not honoring him with a party. The Father came out of his house to meet both brothers where they were. Prodigal went into the house; Elder brother did not. It is God who has always been seeking fellowship with man. He has always been and remains the *waiting Father*. Fellowship between God and man was the Father's idea from the beginning. That was the original purpose of creation. It is our destiny if we dare pursue it. "Rise! Let us go hence" (John 14:31) into the kingdom of God.

Old Testament saints did not know God as Father. That is the reason it was necessary for Jesus to come make him known. Mankind, even those in the nation of Israel, never understood the Fatherhood of God. By coming to the prophets of Israel God offered an ever-increasing insight into his nature. But no one came to see God as Father apart from the ministry of the Son Jesus. Those who did not understand God as Father are the ones who condemned him for blasphemy because of his message. We must not judge them for not knowing; many Christians today still do not know (experience) him as the Father of love. Jesus' prayer of forgiveness from the cross was for those who do not understand what they are doing.

Some See Without Seeing

So, the Baptist recognized the Lamb by observing his walk. That is the sign John put up for us to read. Nicodemus also saw something about Jesus by watching his walk. He came to Jesus and said, "*You are a teacher come from God...No one can do these signs that you do, unless God is with him*" (John 3:2). But Nicodemus missed something. Jesus replied, "*That which is born of the flesh is flesh and that which is born of the Spirit is spirit*" (John 3:6).

Nicodemus saw the *deeds* Jesus did but interpreted them by his human understanding. He failed to follow the arrow by the Spirit. His confession—that God must be with Jesus—was apparently prompted by a logical conclusion rather than by his openness to revelation from the Father. Revelation never comes through flesh and blood, but only from the "Father who is in heaven" (Matt. 16:16). Nicodemus had seen the way Jesus walked as a sign, but he had not seen the sign by the Spirit.

Nicodemus apparently became a disciple. He was the one who questioned the rulers when they were condemning Jesus without a trial (John 7:50). He was also present at the burial of Jesus with Joseph of Arimathea (John 19:39). He was on the right path in chapter three, but he was not yet moving in the right direction. To come to the bosom of the Father we must stay on the path of revelation until we arrive at the destination. Nicodemus stayed on the path; he continued the journey until he found what he was looking for.

When Nicodemus said, "God is with him", he spoke the truth. But Nicodemus had not yet said all that must be said. He had not yet seen all there is to be seen in the relationship between Jesus and his Father. Others had worked miracles in the Old Testament and God was certainly with them in some sense. And it could truly be said of many teachers and prophets that they had come from God. He sent them.

None of these came from God in the same way Jesus came from God. Nor did they walk like *this man* walked. God was with *this man*, and *this man* was with God in a way that was radically new in the world. Jesus was *in* the Father, not merely *with* him, and the Father is in him still today. And if we are in him, we are also in the Father and the Father is in us. Nicodemus spoke as though God was far away. In his mind, Jesus had been sent by this far-away God. He did not see that God was standing in front of him—*The Father in the Son and the Son in the Father.*

Nicodemus had noticed the signs but had not yet accurately followed the pointing finger to find himself in the Father's embrace. What had Nicodemus failed to see? Here is the point. The presence of the Son *IS* the presence of the Father. The daily walk of Jesus issued from his place in the bosom of his Father. More than that, his deeds were the Father's doing: "...*the Father who dwells in me is doing his work*" (John. 14:8-10). Nicodemus had failed to see the Father in the Son and the Son in the Father.

When Jesus said to him, "*...unless one is born again, he cannot see the kingdom of God*" (John. 3:3), Nicodemus thought Jesus was speaking of *motherhood*. The word in Greek for being born can refer to motherhood (giving birth) or to fatherhood (begetting). Nicodemus missed the point. Jesus was referring to *fatherhood*. If one could repeat the motherhood experience, nothing would really change. The seed comes from the father; and *seed reproduces after its own kind*. If you are born of a new seed, you have a new nature.

The word translated *again* can be rendered 'from above' or 'a second time'. Nicodemus thought Jesus was talking about being born a second time. But Jesus was speaking of the possibility of coming into a radically new relationship with God. He was speaking of our becoming sons and daughters, begotten of God the Father (John. 1:13).

We will clarify this in a later chapter. For now, we will just say that God was doing something in the world through the abiding of the Son. The Father was living out his vision through the obedience of the Son. The Son was living his life in total submission to the vision of the Father. If anyone saw the Son walking, he was watching the Father's vision unfold before his very eyes. *That is what Nicodemus had missed.*

Our Commission to Reveal the Father's Love

That is how revelation came to that generation. That is how it comes to our generation as well. When we think of our abiding in the Father's love as being a snuggle-bug in his lap, we miss the point. *Abiding in his love means living in the presence of our neighbor as a manifestation of the Father's love towards them.* As we allow Father to live out his vision through our obedience, we become a revelation of Father's love to our neighbor. Our life becomes an unfolding narrative of God's love for our world.

When he said, "*If you keep my commandments, you will abide in my love, just as I have kept my Father's commandments and abide in his love*" (John. 15:10), he was inviting us to walk in a way that might get us in trouble. In this context, the commands are not those written in the Law, they are the daily instructions the Father gives us. The Father's love will be available to others through our obedience to what he is saying today. The trouble comes because some people are threatened by true love. They have been wounded by a false love and will attack anyone who tries to love them. The religious and political leaders crucified Jesus even though he was Love Incarnate. We are called to follow this love.

The Way: Faith, Love, and Hope

So, our obedience reveals the love of the Father to the degree that it is the same kind of obedience Jesus practiced. It is not an obedience focused on rules and regulations. Jesus simply did what he saw the Father doing. In this way the Father's will became actual in the presence of the community. Obedience is tied to faith, hope, and love. Jesus believed his Father was with him (faith) and lived his life (loved) in the confident expectation (hope) that his Father would do what he promised.

Faith believes—is grasped by—the promise that he will be with you in what you do in response to his prompting. In believing we bind ourselves to him and to his agenda. We allow ourselves to be grasped and carried along in Father's tummy pack.

Love responds to the Spirit's prompting—it will always be a loving response because God is love.

Hope looks forward to the fulfillment of the promise knowing that the Father will do what he said he would do.

The faith, love, and hope that reveal the Father is simply walking in obedience toward the fulfillment of the promised presence of the Father and the Son in us, with us, and through us.

"*He who abides in him ought to walk in the same way in which he walked*" (I John. 2:6). The word "*way*" indicates a significant concept in the New Testament. The early Church was simply called *the Way* (Acts 9:2). The Church is the *Way* only as it follows Jesus who is THE WAY. A disciple is in the *Way* only as he follows Jesus and walks in the same *way* Jesus walked. The *way* he walked revealed the Father's love for the world. Our *way* should also be a way that reveals Father's love to our world.

This Way was revealed on the third day, the day of transition from the old creation to the new creation.

The Transition Begins

"*The two disciples heard him say this.*" When John gave his testimony, probably many disciples were with him. Many certainly must have heard the words of his testimony, but their hearing did not affect their walk. Some of those sent by the scribes and Pharisees may also have been in the crowd. Only two men *heard* the testimony on this third day and began their walk along that path.

How could anyone really hear that testimony without turning to follow? If they heard without following, it makes one wonder if they really heard. This dilemma is solved when we distinguish between a hearing through what you already have in your mind and a hearing that pops your balloon. Two disciples who were there on this third day really did hear. They allowed their mental bias to be challenged.

Someone heard. Someone was *present* to the sign. Someone turned and began to follow the pointing finger. This third day is the beginning of the transition from the Old Testament prophets, John being the last. The focus of biblical history is shifting to *this man* Jesus.

Two Disciples Followed

"*And they followed Jesus.*" The decrease of the Baptist's ministry began here. John just lost two disciples. Later when a number of John's other disciples leave him to follow Jesus, those who remained with John said, "*Rabbi, he who was with you beyond the Jordan, to whom you bore witness, here he is, baptizing, and all are going to him*" (John. 3:26). These loyal disciples of the Baptist were concerned that he might lose his following. But their concern was not John's concern. John had testified, "*...for this I came baptizing with water, that he might be revealed to Israel*" (John. 1:31). The

Baptist knew he was not the light. He had come to bear witness to the light.

So, the Baptist was not surprised or disappointed when his disciples began to leave him to follow Jesus. For him, the transition was natural. This nonpartisan attitude was evident in his response to those remaining disciples: *"No one can receive anything except what is given him from heaven"* (John. 3:27). Those who are given to Jesus will turn and follow Jesus. Those who are given! John was not like a controlling pastor who is jealous and possessive over those who gather themselves around him. If God had given them to him, God could also take them away.

When these two began to turn from him toward Jesus, the Baptist was pleased to know they were hearing his testimony. *"He who has the bride is the bridegroom; the friend of the bridegroom, who stands and hears him, rejoices greatly at the bridegroom's voice; therefore, this joy of mine is now full"* (John. 3:29).

The real surprise is that John did not insist that all his disciples follow Jesus. Why did he let anyone continue with him after he identified the Lord? Because it was not his job to *send* disciples to Jesus; his only task was to bear witness to what he had seen. No one can come to the Son unless the Father draws him (John. 6:44). The Baptist was at ease with those who stayed, and he was at ease with those who went. Love does not control.

We find the same candor in Jesus when he asks the twelve, *"Do you also wish to go away?"* (John. 6:67). Those who were with him were not forced to remain when others were leaving. There was no pressure from Jesus, and there was no pressure from the Baptist. If you *hear*, you will follow. If you *really* hear, you will continue to follow when Jesus goes in a direction you do not expect.

The Significance of These Two

The Baptist's remaining disciples had not yet seen what he saw. They had heard the *words* of the testimony, but they had not yet heard the *voice* of Father; the words did not register in their hearts. They saw the *man* the Baptist was pointing to, but they did not see the *Lamb of God*. They heard the words from John's mouth, but they missed the voice pointing beyond the natural to the unseen realm. Since they had neither heard nor seen what needs to be heard and seen, they were still disciples of the Baptist.

Two disciples of John did follow. They followed because they had heard a sound from above, a voice bearing the words. The vibrations of that voice entered their hearts and resonated with what was there. With them the historical transition from the Baptist to Jesus had its beginning. The events that took place as they followed will help us in our quest to discover what it means to follow Jesus as a true disciple. Our first clue lies in the question Jesus asks them: "What do you seek?"

The exchange between these two disciples and Jesus will be the guiding principle for the next chapters. We mentioned in chapter one that John introduced topics in one place and expanded them in other places in his Gospel. We draw attention to that again here and we will demonstrate it more clearly in the following meditations. It is as if the seeds for the whole Gospel are present in the four days of this first chapter. This will become more obvious as we read each story and each exchange as a *sign* pointing beyond itself to the ultimate reality of the relationship between the Father and the Son as they bring salvation to the world.

We ask again, does our obedience reveal the love of God to our generation? Can others tell by the way we walk that we have an abiding place in the Father? Can they tell we are in him and he is in us? Can we honestly say concerning our work that he who abides in us is doing his work? Can we say with Paul, "It is no longer I who live but Christ who lives in me?" (Gal. 2:20). That is what it means to follow *this man* and walk this Way. Has this historical transition affected our way of relating to friends and foes?

In the next chapter we will explore the question, "*What do you seek?*" That is the question Jesus asked the two disciples of John who heard the testimony and followed Jesus. It is a question that comes to everyone who leaves a former commitment to follow Jesus. What we seek determines what we might find.

Each of the questions and responses recorded in this third day are echoed in other places in the Gospel of John. When we bring them together, the arrow of the pointing signs will begin to emerge. There is a story or dialogue specifically designed to open the meaning of each of the elements in this exchange between Jesus and these first two disciples. As we delve into the context of these stories and dialogues, the integrity of the Gospel should become clear.

We should keep in mind, however, that the focus should not be on these two disciples as individuals. These two men are signs pointing to every true disciple. We will be looking at principles that apply to every disciple who turns from where he was and begins to follow Jesus to where he is going. Many personal applications will come to light.

We are now ready for the question, "What do you seek?" Be ready to take that question personally. What are you looking for in life?

Chapter Seven
What Do You Seek?

We have learned that the third day indicated the transition from the Old to the New. On that day, the old was passing and the new was coming. That transition was marked by two of the Baptist's disciples who heard his testimony and saw by the Spirit what the Baptist had seen. They saw the way Jesus walked and sensed something that caused them to turn and follow Jesus. They were following because of who he is, not because of what he might give them. They were beginning a journey toward the bosom of the Father although they did not yet have a clue what that meant.

My Personal Journey

The desire for intimacy with the Father had no place in my early Christian walk. My earthly father was an abusive alcoholic during my pre-teen and teen years. There was no possibility of intimacy with him. I avoided him as much as possible during in those years.

I accepted Jesus in the summer of 1945, just before my ninth birthday. Jesus was my daily companion and my friend. But the thought of seeking a relationship with his Father was foreign to me. I thought he would be like my dad.

The Father's Love

In 1957, in the spring before my twenty-first birthday, God came to me in an Air Force barrack in Japan. I was immersed in his love for over an hour. The only way I can describe the experience is to say the room filled with liquid love; I was overwhelmed by (baptized in) Love. From that day to this my heart pants for intimacy with him, even though I do experience times of complacency. Having this intimacy as both an experience and as a goal has made the journey from isolation to intimacy exciting, rewarding, and bearable.

Interpreting the Experience

At first, I interpreted that experience in Japan as Jesus coming to me and affirming his love for me despite the life I was living at that time. Having been immersed in liquid love, I was on a spiritual high for several years before I became complacent. Later, when the Charismatic renewal and the Jesus Movement broke into history, I interpreted the liquid love experience as the Baptism of the Holy Spirit. I began to seek a deeper level of intimacy with God again. He visited me again and again during that time of learning to breath in the atmosphere of Love.

Another period of complacency set in. When the teaching of the Father's love became popular among God's people, I interpreted my experience in Japan as the Father coming to me with the love I never received from my dad. I began to seek him even more earnestly. He has visited me several times since. With each visit I become more intense in my hunger and panting after him. Each new experience of his presence sparked a personal revival of seeking for more.

All three interpretations were correct: the liquid love of the Father, Son and Holy Spirit came to me in that Air Force barrack. His love came more profoundly each time I moved forward in my pilgrimage toward the Father's bosom. I know there is more of that love waiting for me in the future and I continue to thirst for greater and greater fulfillment. This upward spiral never ends because there is always more to God than what any of us have seen or received.

Seeking and Finding

We all experience life like a pendulum of seeking and finding and seeking again.

A search generally ends when we find what we are looking for. But if it is God we are seeking, we experience our human ambiguity in the process. We fear God and we desire him at the same time. "Fear God and keep his commandments," we are told. We are also instructed, "Love the Lord thy God with all your heart, soul, mind and strength." When the angel of the Lord showed up, his first words were always, "Fear not," because he recognized our human ambiguity. We chase after him, then run away from him.

Our journey into the bosom of the Father can be compared to being drawn upward on a spiral staircase, going around in circles but attaining a higher level with each cycle. I say "being drawn upward" to indicate it is not our human effort that takes us to the next level. To use another metaphor, it becomes like a dance with continual movement back and forth, in and out, up, and around, with

Jesus taking the lead in the dance. Add to this image (of a spiral staircase or a dance) the concept of abiding in God and a pattern emerges:

We fear we will be absorbed or destroyed by an increased presence of God, so we pull away. Many who call themselves atheists fall into this category. It is easier to deny God than to face God.

We hear a word—perhaps a word of testimony from one who has experienced a deeper measure of God's love than we have. Or we may have an experience of some new dimension of God's love. That is what happened to me in Japan. We are captivated by that word or that experience.

We become aware of a deep hunger that has always been in our hearts all along. The word (or the experience) awakens us to the possibility of something more satisfying than what we have experienced so far.

We seek more of the love we experienced or heard about with fresh enthusiasm.

When we seek, we find. We experience the Father's love on a deeper level. If that presence is especially heavy, we desire it but also want it to lift. We feel like we might die if it continues.

We overcome the fear of being absorbed or destroyed by his presence, then grow accustomed to this new level of relationship. We forget we are on a higher level than we were and become complacent. Life loses its vitality and we become bored. Someone said, "I did not realize how boring church was till God showed up."

We hear another word, recognize that there is more, we seek more earnestly, we experience more of his love, overcome the fear, and abide more profoundly. Then we become accustomed to the new level only to discover there is even more…and the dance continues.

Two disciples heard John's testimony, *"Behold the Lamb of God."* They recognized a deep hunger in their hearts and began to follow Jesus. Their exciting journey of seeking and finding had just begun! They had only begun to follow Jesus when he popped the question: *"What do you seek?"* In this chapter we focus on that question. As we continue to pursue an understanding of what it means to follow Jesus into the Father's embrace, we are all encouraged to hear it as a question addressed to each of us personally. "What do you seek?"

The goal of being in an intimate relationship with *Abba* ("Daddy God") gives meaning to the journey. That goal also gives courage to face the difficulties we meet on the road as we follow Jesus. The vision of a future with deeper and deeper experiences of love keeps us moving forward. If we experience reality, our memory of past failures loses its influence because of the power of our new vision of the future. However, if we only find increased information, the past pain continues to pull us backward.

We are all somewhere on the road between alienation and continual intimacy with God. Between here and there we have difficult times and times of glorious experiences with him. Sometimes the difficulties come because we are looking for something which is not available except in our imagination. There is always more of God than we have received even in the most glorious experiences, but that 'more' may not be what we are thinking. As we move forward, the way becomes easier if we remember the goal: receiving more of Father God's love and passing it on to others.

Ponder this possibility: *what we seek may determine and limit what we are able to find.* Once again, the picture in our imagination can prejudice our vision and our hearing. If we seek one who matches our expectation, we will be exposed as confused disciples when Jesus makes a turn that does not show up on our radar. When life takes an unexpected turn, it is important to remember who we are following and where he is leading us—into Father's embrace and then out from that embrace into the world with his love for others.

Take Heed How You Hear

"*What do you seek?*" We all must answer this question before we can approach the true Way. When Jesus saw two of the Baptist's disciples following him, he asked that question. It has an almost confrontational quality to it: "I need to know what you are looking for so I can know how to respond to you. What you are really after will determine whether I make myself and my resources available to you." Obviously, Jesus was not out to gain a big following.

He knew many would follow him through the geographical countryside. Many of them would be chasing their own dreams and would try to force him to conform to the images in their mind's eye. Jesus wanted these two disciples to consider whether they had preconceived notions of what they expected him to be for them. Beneath Jesus' question is a deeper question, "What have you actually heard?" Their answer to Jesus' question will tell him what they heard and what they are looking for.

How we hear and how we see determines our spiritual journey. Noise from the expectations in our balloon can filter out the sound of heaven. The natural light of our human intellect can prejudice our vision. If we do not hear the message right, we draw wrong conclusions and expect something Jesus is not offering. What we are ready to hear is indicated by what we are seeking when we come to him. Often what we hear is not what was said. Husbands and wives know this situation well.

There was probably a lot of talk around the community when Jesus showed up in town. Everyone who heard or saw him filtered their experience through their personal desires and expectations. Each generated his or her own report through his or her preconceived notions. What our heart desires will filter how we listen and what we hear. We begin to expect Jesus to fulfill our desire; but we may be seeking something that has nothing to do with what Jesus is offering.

It becomes a giant game of "whisper down the lane" as people talk about *this man* who just came to town. That is why Jesus said, "Take heed how you hear" (Lk. 8:18), and that is why he asks, "*What do you seek?*" The biblical concept of hearing includes the idea of a positive response to what is said. To hear is to agree and join the one speaking; it means to follow him on his journey. We may hear the words without desiring to join the disciples who follow, or we may hear through our filter and join the journey for the wrong reason. Neither of these are the kind of hearing that results in an intimate relationship with the one who asked.

We see the same type of challenge in Jesus' response to the rich young ruler in Matthew 19:16-22. This young man knew something was missing in his life. He had heard a report about Jesus that made him think Jesus could help him find what he was seeking. He wanted eternal life (remember that eternal life in that society meant a good, prosperous life here and now) and he thought Jesus had the answer, so he asked, "What do I still lack?" He knew something was missing in his life here and now. Jesus said, "Sell what you possess and give to the poor and you will have treasures in heaven; and come, follow me."

Walking away sad, the young man exposed himself as one who was not willing to let go of his possessions. That was not the image of eternal life he had in his balloon. It was not a word he was willing to hear. He was probably thinking, "What is the value of treasures in heaven if I have to leave my earthly treasures behind while I am here?" He wanted both eternal life and earthly treasures. But he wanted the earthly treasures more! He was not giving heed to how he was hearing Jesus. He understood the words all too well but was not willing to follow under those conditions.

Jesus did not chase him or try to make him change his mind. Jesus was not willing to adjust his message or agenda to accommodate any of those who wanted to follow him. He would let them go another way if they were not willing to let the images in their mental backpack dissolve. Love (God) does not control. Love knows that control breeds rebellion.

Take Heed What You Hear

Mark's Gospel recorded Jesus' interpretation of the parable of the sower in a slightly different way from Luke. In Mark we read, "Take heed *what* you hear." The shift from "how" to "what" is significant, but it carries the same message. We noticed above that the biblical concept of hearing includes a positive response to the one speaking. In Mark we see the same principle from a different perspective.

Hearing is involved in the development of our concepts of God, the world, and ourselves. What we heard from our parents and other important people involved in our early training influenced the way we see life. We see life through the lens given with those words from others. In other words, our imaging faculty is filled with things we have heard, and our present life is flowing out from what is in our heart through what we heard (Prov. 4:23). What we hear in our adult life will also influence how we see ourselves, how we see the world, how we see God. What we hear influences how we respond to life.

We must pay attention to the words that are spoken in our presence because words have the power to create either death or life (Prov. 18:21). When we allow words to enter our heart (our balloon), we are giving those words a place of influence in our life. This is what James called receiving with meekness the implanted word (Js. 1:21). To receive a word with meekness means to allow that word to take the reins of our life and lead us. By the time we are adults we have already received with meekness many words spoken by important others in our life.

So, the question of what we seek is tied to the question of what we have heard. We look for that which we have learned to value. We value what others have told us is good. By the time we are middle aged we have usually discovered that some of the things we thought were good turned out to be destructive. Difficulties and failures in life are invitations to hear the question again: "What do you seek; what do you expect to have in your hands at the end of this journey."

What we seek is also tied to what we are presently hearing with meekness. When things are not going well, we listen for insights on how to do life differently. We begin to listen for another word to save us from the mess we have made. This brings the issue to our daily life.

Here is the process in a nutshell:

1. We receive a word from someone.

2. We expect life to reward us according to the word we received.

3. We seriously seek after what we think has ultimate value.

4. When what we treasure turns out to be a curse, we are in a place to hear a different word with a different promise from a different person.

5. What we hear determines what we seek after, and what we seek after determines what we can see. In other words, what we are looking for prejudices our seeking and our seeing.

What we seek determines what we are prepared to receive from the Father through Jesus the Son. I was not prepared to receive anything from the Father because I thought he was like my dad. The implications of this concept will become clear as we look at the three categories of people John the Baptist addressed. That will be the topic of our next chapter.

We Must Each Answer This Question

Jesus addressed this question to each of us as we follow him. We must hear this question if we are beginning to follow him for the first time. We must hear it again each time we return to follow with a deeper commitment: "What do you expect to find by following me?" We must hear it again daily: "What are you after? What do you hope to have in your hands at the end of this journey? What expectations do you believe I have come to fulfill?"

It is crucial for us to hear the questions in a radical way because what we expect at the end of the journey indicates whether we are beginning to follow Jesus or the image of the Christ in our balloon. As disciples we learn on the way that Jesus did not come to fulfill our human vision. He is out to empty our mental backpack and fill it with himself and his mission.

The Lord makes himself available to us based on what we are seeking. That does not mean he will give us whatever we want. "Seek and you will find" (Lk. 11:9) is not simply a promise that anyone who thinks he is seeking God will find the true God, at least not in the sense in which that is usually understood. This is clear from what Jesus said to the Pharisees, "*You will seek me, and you will not find me*" (John 7:34). One kind of seeking finds God, but the other kind does not. Fullness of life depends on how we hear and what we hear. What we hear forms our attitudes and motives. How we hear influences our willingness or unwillingness to move beyond the preconceived notions that govern our expectations.

If our attitude is one of humility, we will be open for the Lord to challenge the images in our minds. If our motive is to establish ourselves in the way we have chosen, we will continue to insist that reality conform to our preconceived notions. It never will, so we are wasting our time, wasting our life if we keep trying.

Chapter Eight
Three Classes of People

The first three days of transition from the Baptist to Jesus represent three classes of people. John's testimony was different on each day because he addressed a different group each day. Each group was seeking something quite different because each group had heard reports of Jesus' ministry differently. Some heard the reports as a threat to their position in the community, some heard them as a promise of the fulfillment of their own goals and dreams, and some heard the report as a word from above. What have you heard?

Just as The Baptist saw Jesus with the seeing eye of a prophet, he also discerned the condition of his audience with sensitivity to the Spirit. John did not formally ask the question, "What are you seeking?" before he testified to each group, but the question with its challenge was hovering in the atmosphere over each audience as he gave his testimony. That same question is still hovering over us today.

The Baptist perceived the unspoken answer to the unspoken question and testified to each group appropriately. He spoke to the spiritual condition of those present in his audience. He did not have a canned testimony; he was not passing out tracts; he was not repeating the same words to everyone. Each group's unspoken answer to the question was a barometer of the spiritual condition of the audience. Their answer determined the content of John's testimony as well as their ability to receive or reject that testimony.

Let us look at each group separately. We will draw attention to the difference in the Baptist's message to each group and infer from each message what the attitudes and motives behind each group's responses might be.

The First Group: Self-Seekers

The first group (John 1:19-28) was made up of a delegation of priests and Levites from the Jewish leaders in Jerusalem. They asked John, "*Who are you?*" They had come to investigate him, to measure him and his message by the standards of their human court. Perhaps they were angry or threatened because the crowds considered him a spiritual leader or even a prophet. We gather from John's Gospel and from the other Gospels that they did not think God sent him.

They probably wanted to discredit the Baptist. They had their own ideas about how a man of God ought to dress and what he ought to teach. They had clear notions of what *ought* to happen when God moves. John was not doing any of those things right as far as this audience was concerned. He did not have credentials acceptable to these self-appointed religious leaders. The Baptist knew he could never measure up to their expectations. He did not even try because he was not commissioned to please them.

They were looking for *their* Messiah and they were quite sure he would reveal himself to them first. They were certain that they would recognize Messiah without help from other men, especially from a madman in the desert like the Baptist. They would never ask a man like that to point them in the right direction. These religious leaders' answer to the question, "What do you seek," would not satisfy Jesus who was behind the scene asking. The Baptist discerned their attitude, so he did not cooperate with them. They were seeking the wrong things for the wrong reasons because they had not heard from above. They had only heard from earth (John 3:31-32).

Always Right

People who are always right in their own eyes are seldom open to the testimony of others unless it agrees with what they already think they know. They are blind to what is right in front of their eyes unless it compares favorably to their preconceived notions. They do not ask or seek with an openness to hear or see anything that might contradict their understanding of truth. They come only as teachers or judges, never as students or disciples. They come as those who already know, not as those seeking.

Those religious leaders were not seeking God. They were seeking to establish their superiority over others. They were not willing to go beyond the preconceived notions that govern their expectations. They only wanted the security they found in their balloons. Balloons pop easily so they had built strong doctrinal walls and powerful political structures to protect the supposed superiority of their prejudices. Many of those became controllers and tried to bind everyone else to their ideas and practices.

The Negative Testimony

"*I am not the Christ.*" In the last chapter we suggested that the Baptist should have continued, "There he is over there! He is the one you are looking for." But he did not point. He made no attempt to take them beyond their present understanding. He knew they were not seeking the one to whom he had been sent to bear witness. He left them in their blindness just as Jesus would later do with the Pharisees (John 9).

The Baptist was not uptight about getting those men to see what he had come to show. He was at ease with the fact that the Father was not giving these men a positive witness about the Son. When they asked if he was Elijah or the prophet, he was satisfied simply to answer that he was not the one they were looking for.

"*Among you stands one whom you do not know,*" John continued. As they continued to press for answers, he did give them something like a testimony. He indicated that the one he came to identify was among them even though they did not recognize him. We can capture the significance of this moment by reading between the lines:

John implied, "The one you *ought* to be seeking is out there if you only had eyes to see! He is among you, but he is there as one whom you do not know. I cannot show you who he is because you are looking for the wrong thing. You are only seeking confirmation of your own human ideas. I could point in his direction, but you are blinded by your own arrogance so you would not see him for who he is anyway. I could speak all the right words, but you would never hear my testimony because you are deaf to anything that does not agree with what you think you already know. So, you do not know who he is, and I am not at liberty to point him out to you at this time."

Pride Is the Problem

These inquisitors were coming to the Baptist—as the Pharisees would later come to Jesus—for the wrong reasons. If Jesus had asked the Pharisees "*What are you seeking?*" they would likely have given some high-sounding answer to give the impression they were seeking God. But even though they put on airs of seeking God, they were really seeking their own glory (John 5:44). Since Jesus knew what was in their mental backpack, *he did not trust himself to them* (John 2:24-25). He refused to play their religious game. That is why they wanted to kill him.

The Gospel of John referred to this group as *the Jews.* John positioned them throughout the book as a sign of all those (Jew or Gentile) who opposed the ministry of Jesus and challenge his teaching based on their own religious ideas. They kept trying to arrest him and to restrict his movement. They never really heard what he was saying. They heard the words but missed the voice with its hidden message. They saw the deeds but missed the signs.

These self-appointed, self-seeking leaders were out to kill Jesus from the beginning because he would not conform to their preconceived notions of how a man of God ought to behave. The way he was walking was not the way they expect the Messiah to walk. John presented these men as signs of all those who insist on their own way.

They did not have this difficulty because they were Jews. Their difficulty came from being human beings who were not open to see beyond their own preconceived notions. In their pride they thought they knew God. They did not engage in any serious seeking because they thought they had already found the prize. They thought they knew so they only engaged in 'proof-texting' to defend the god they already had in their bubble. I use the lower case for *god* because the god these religious leaders knew was not the true God. The god they knew was not the Father of Jesus Christ the Son. Their god did not have a son.

Jesus later said to these men, "*You know neither me nor my Father; if you knew me, you would know my Father also*" (John. 8:19). No wonder they wanted to kill him. He dared to suggest they did not know God.

Two Kinds of Blindness

This same group cast the blind man out of the synagogue when he testified that Jesus had healed him. They must cast out the one God healed to defend the god of their imagination. In effect, they cast God out with the man. Their blindness was worse than his blindness. They were blind to their own blindness. This is the nature of self-deception; your deception deceives you. Jesus said of them, "*if you were blind, you would have no guilt; but now that you say, 'We see,' your guilt remains*" (John. 9:41). Guilt will always remain on those who are not willing to see their own sin, who only focus on the sins of others.

There are none as blind as those who refuse to look because they think they already see.

So, the basic problem of the scribes and Pharisees is that they are seeking the wrong god. If you ask them, they will insist that they are among the few who are really seeking God. But the god they are seeking is the god of their own religious imagination, the one that exists only in their imagination. If this religious god of theirs had a son, that son would obviously agree with them and affirm their right to have religious power, authority, and superiority.

They do not have ears to hear anything that disagrees with what they have already determined as truth. These religious leaders carry the same spirit of superiority found in the devil himself. Jesus revealed their critical condition when they claimed that God was their Father. "*If God were your Father,*" Jesus responded, "*you would love me, for I proceeded and came forth from God…. You are of your father the devil.*" (John 8:42-44)

In choosing a path that promised to bring glory to themselves, they were walking in a way that leads to death with no resurrection. This is not the Way of Jesus Christ.

The seriousness of this question becomes painfully apparent. If you are seeking the wrong thing you are on the wrong path; and the wrong path leads in the wrong direction. This is a spiral that goes downward, a dance that ends in the pit. If you refuse to let your religious ideas be challenged, God's appointed witness will be mute, and you will never even know you are on the wrong path. "There is a way which seems right to a man, but its end is the way to death" (Prov. 4:12). May God save us from ourselves!

Pride Is Still With Us Today

These leaders are still among us today. They exalt themselves among God's people as judges and executioners. They use the "sword of the Spirit" to deride and defame those who disagree with them. They step into a revival to stamp out the fire that comes to those who receive newness. They try to arrest and restrict the movement of the Spirit within the community of God's people.

They do not literally kill, but with gossip and slander they come against those who are open to what God is presently doing. Jesus addressed this attitude when he gave commentary on the commandment, "You shall not kill." He said, "...everyone who is angry with his brother shall be liable to judgment; whoever insults his brother shall be liable to the council, and whoever says, 'You fool!' is liable to hell fire" (Matt. 5:22).

Some leaders reject the possibility that God might move outside the circle of their influence or beyond the borders of their personal kingdom. Surely God would not even consider doing anything without checking with them first. They never hear the testimony of others except for the sake of a doctrinal debate. They are too focused on themselves and their programs to listen to anyone. There is always someone standing among them whom they do not know and do not understand, and that someone must be silenced at any price.

Leaders and Followers

None of us is exempt from the question, "*What do you seek?*" It is easy for those of us who are not in leadership to think our leaders do not hear from God because they do not agree with us. When we discredit a worship leader, are we seeking to establish God's way or our own way? Are we trying to get others to think we know more about worship than the worship leader? We can debunk the pastor for debunking others. When we do, are we not doing the same things? Do we think our ability to see what is wrong with the youth leader make us superior? Even if we have seen clearly, is criticism and backbiting the proper response?

That desire to appear superior is the same thing that motivates leaders to criticize and expel those who disagree with them. The only difference is that they have the position of power and we do not. When it is time to confront our leaders, we should make sure the Father's love is prompting every motive, evert attitude, every word, and every action. The inappropriate criticism of leadership is just as destructive to the community of believers as dominating leaders are. What do you seek?

I was with a group of church leaders on a retreat. We invited several young men to join us to give them the opportunity to learn something about leadership. During one of the breaks one young man came to me privately and began to criticize some of the processes and the decisions the leaders were making. He may have been right, but I sensed he was trying to impress me with his deep insight. When he told me what he would have done if he were an elder, I said, "Perhaps that's why God has not made you and elder." He got the point and received the correction. That humble response was his first step to becoming the leader God called him to be.

One cannot cast out pride with pride. When we criticize leadership, it is often because we want to lead but are not willing to carry the cross of leadership. We just stir up trouble trying to manipulate the leader to do it our way. This feels safe because if things go wrong the burden will be on the leader who made the decision; it will not be on our shoulders. We are not following Jesus when we do that. We are seeking something other than an intimate relationship with Father. Jesus humbled himself so that others could be exalted to the Father's bosom. We should walk as he walked—in humility.

If the Body of Christ calls you a leader, Jesus calls you to follow him as a servant to those you lead. "Wash one another's feet," he said to the twelve leaders he had chosen. If you are not called to leadership, Jesus calls you to follow him as a servant to your leader. Each person is responsible to present his own motives, attitudes, words, and actions to the Lord for judgment. If we are judging others, it is because we are seeking our own kingdom.

The Second Group: The Crowd of Sensation-Seekers

The Baptist addressed a second group the next day (John 1:29-34). In his witness to the group of the second day he presented Jesus as the one who meets the needs of mankind: *"Behold, the Lamb of God who takes away the sin of the world."* This reflects Jesus' ability and willingness to deal with our past failures. The Baptist's testimony continued, *"I saw the Spirit descend as a dove from heaven, and it remained on him.... This is he who baptizes with the Holy Spirit."* He affirmed Jesus' ability to offer us a new future; with the Holy Spirit we will be able to move forward in victory.

This testimony was addressed to the public, the multitude, the world Jesus came to save. The judgmental Jews of the previous day may have been in the crowd, but they could not *hear* this message without giving up their feeling of superiority. The Apostle John is probably posting a sign that reads: "This announcement is for the whole world!" The Baptist was saying to the uncommitted crowd gathered to see this new thing in the desert, "All of the blessings of God are available to you through *this man* to whom I am now pointing."

The Crowd of Unbelieving Believers

We can understand the condition of the crowd by looking at John 2:23-24: *"Now when he was in Jerusalem at the Passover feast, many* [the crowd] *believed in his name when they saw the signs which he did; but Jesus did not trust himself to them."* Here is an important observation from the Greek. The word translated "believe" and the word translated "trust" is the same word. These verses could be translated, "many trusted themselves to him, but he did not trust himself to them," or "many believed in him, but he did not believe in them." He did not commit himself to what they were committed to! They had a picture in their imagination that was not true to reality. Jesus did not respond to their believing the way they expected him to respond. He did not *bind himself* to their agenda.

Expecting a Superhero: Thatman!

If we understand the context, we can feel the full impact of these statements. The crowd saw the signs Jesus did in Jerusalem. They saw him as a candidate to fulfill their messianic dreams and hopes. He was "*Thatman*"—the Christ in their balloon who swings down from above to do violence to their enemies! "With *Thatman's* powers on our side," some may have said among themselves, "we can march in, drive the Romans into the sea, and have political freedom again. What a way of life it would be with *Thatman* as king. He can heal all our diseases and give us daily bread. With *Thatman*, life would be wonderful. We would have no problems; he would fix everything. And who knows, maybe he will let me be Robin, the boy wonder!" Jesus saw this movie playing on the screen of their hearts and said, "I am NOT *Thatman*!"

In so many subtle ways they might have come to Jesus and said, "We recognize you as a man who can fulfill our dreams. We will trust ourselves and all our resources to you. You can be our leader.

We have informers in significant places that can monitor the moves of the enemy. We have swords and men trained in guerilla warfare. All this we will make available to you so you can lead us the way we want to go. You can accomplish our agenda for us. You can take over the program we have put together and take us toward our goals. How could you pass up a deal like that?"

Their answer to the critical question, "*What do you seek?*" is formulating before Jesus' eyes. They are seeking their own success, their own way, and their own comfort. They are seeking to establish themselves as the people of God without any change in their hearts. They are self-seeking at the core of their being. Jesus was (and still is) seeking those who are seeking an active abiding relationship in the bosom of Father God. Self-seekers appear to be seeking God only to others who are also self-seekers.

Jesus' simple response would be. "You would trust yourselves and your resources to me to accomplish your will; but my will is not your will. I did not come to drive the Romans out. I came to bring them into the Kingdom of God. I came to establish my Father's Kingdom, not your kingdom. I will trust neither myself nor my resources to you because I am bound in faithfulness to my Father and his mission. The military leader you want is not the leader I came to be. I have a campaign assigned to me by my Father and I only do what pleases him."

Feeding the Multitude

We see the *crowd of the second day* in the feeding of the multitude story. After Jesus had provided the meal, while the disciples were collecting the leftovers, the people began to reflect on what had happened, saying, "*This is indeed the prophet who is coming into the world*" (John 6:14). They believed in him and were ready to commit themselves to him, but they only wanted him to be their leader because they thought *Thatman* would fulfill their dreams.

They had not yet seen him for who he is. All they knew was that *Thatman*—the one in their head—could make life easy for them. They had seen the feeding of the multitude as a sign, but they thought the sign was pointing to the Christ in the movie of their fantasy—the one with unlimited wealth and power to destroy the Romans.

The phrase "*the prophet who is coming into the world*" reflected their understanding of an ancient prophecy that God would raise up a prophet like Moses from among the people (Deut. 18:15). The popular interpretation of that text was that a man of God would appear who, like Moses, would provide manna for their journey. People believed that in this utopia all man's needs would be met supernaturally. There would be economic abundance without work. Who would not want a king like that? With the miracle of the feeding of the multitude it was natural for them to conclude that Jesus was *Thatman*.

Jesus Withdrew Himself

The text continues, "*Perceiving then that they were about to come and take him by force to make him king, Jesus withdrew again to the mountain by himself*" (John. 6:15). Here we see the same response from Jesus as in John 2:23-24. They believe in Jesus, but he does not believe in them. He would not trust himself or his resources to them in a way that would give their bubble control of the situation.

The king they wanted is not the king he came to be. He did not withhold bread from them even though he knew they were only seeking natural bread. He simply removed *himself* from their presence so they would not be able to force their agenda on him. I wonder how often Jesus withdraws himself from churches today for the same reason. Is that the reason Jesus stands at the door of the church knocking (Rev. 3:20), waiting for someone inside to hear the knock and invite him into their "secret place" for fellowship?

The crowd was not prepared to receive the reality he came to offer. They withdrew from him when he explained that he was offering *himself* to them as the Bread of Life. Jesus, knowing what was in man, had already withdrawn himself from them. He knew what they were seeking, and he refused to let them get at the resources available to him from his Father. Those resources are only available to accomplish the Father's will. They are not available to fulfill human dreams.

They could have had his presence and all those resources as well if they had been willing to allow their heart's desire to be adjusted. If they had been willing to come under his agenda and let him change them, all things would have been available to them—but only for the purpose of the Kingdom of Father God.

The Triumphal Entry

The theme of Jesus withdrawing from the crowd also emerges in the triumphal entry (John 12:12ff.). The crowd went out to meet him because they had heard about the raising of Lazarus from the dead. A sensational ministry always attracts a crowd of people seeking sensations. This crowd was not coming out to Jesus because he was the Lamb of God but because of the sensational thing he had done in their midst. Like the bread-seekers, they were seeking the '*bread*' that would feed their hunger for excitement. They would never get on the field to play the game; they were satisfied to watch from the bleachers. Their desire was to be in the crowd when "our team" wins the game.

Later, when he speaks of his coming death, the crowd chimes in, "*We have heard from the law that the Christ remains forever. How can you say that the Son of Man must be lifted up?*" (John 12:34). Rather than receiving him and remaining to discover what he meant by that, they challenged him. They had not perceived the meaning of Lazarus' resurrection. Most of those in the crowd had a doctrine of resurrection, but it was a doctrine imprisoned within the walls of their synagogues. (Like the "Spirit that raised Jesus from the dead" is held hostage in some church buildings. He is not expected do anything outside.) When you do not *really* believe in resurrection you have to have a Messiah who never dies. You can have *Thatman* only behind closed doors.

They were not willing to follow him unless he would do things according to their preconceived notions. When they challenged his word, we might guess they had already withdrawn themselves from him inwardly. We should not be surprised when we read that Jesus "*...departed and hid himself from them*" (John 12:36). Withdrawal is usually mutual. Jesus withdraws from those who have withdrawn from who he really is. But, having withdrawn, Jesus remains available to those who might come to see later.

The question continues to confront the multitude: "What do you seek?" Here again, the *crowd* exposed as those seeking a fulfillment of their human vision. They were not open to have the content of their religious concepts challenged.

The Crowd Is Still With Us

In every generation this second group appears as the many who follow a sensational ministry with the hope of seeing or experiencing a miracle. They are seeking the thrills, the chills, and the goosebumps. They may get what they want but they have no way to discern between the work of a man with a "goose-bump ministry" and a real move of God. They do not know the difference between *Thatman* and *This Man*.

The saddest thing is that they do not even notice that *Jesus has withdrawn himself* from them. Why should they notice? He is not the one they were seeking. They have found what they were looking for. They have their reward—goosebumps and thrills—so they go away looking for another meeting to attend.

Today's crowd also tries to bind Jesus to their own agenda. They try to force him into the humanized mold of a god who makes life easy and comfortable for them. I call this a *featherbed mentality*. They act as though the call to discipleship is, "Come, let me give you a featherbed (not a cross), and follow me in comfort and leisure. Let me establish your superiority over other men (and especially over women, or over men if you are a woman) so that you will be the all-important one."

They conceive of God as some sort of heavenly Santa Claus who exists to serve their "inner child". This god is only there to fulfill the Great American Dream of pleasure and prosperity. Like the rich young ruler, those seeking this kind of Christ have trouble hearing the invitation, "Sell all you have, give it to the poor, and come follow me. Give up your desire for personal comfort and walk this way with me." It is no wonder they get caught up in the rat race of church power struggles, personal pleasure trips, and programs of self-promotion.

Is it any wonder that the great majority (97% according to statistics) of converts from those methods backslide shortly after they make their commitment? The question keeps hovering in the atmosphere even today: "*What do you seek?*"

Some evangelists have recognized (consciously or unconsciously) this self-serving tendency in our culture and capitalize on it to gain a large following. "Come to Jesus because he will heal you, make you prosperous, and take you to heaven when you die." The promises of God are sure, and he is faithful to fulfill his word. But if people only come for the blessings with no interest in a serious commitment, they will just go somewhere else when Jesus begins to make demands on their lives.

Pastors sometimes try to attract the crowd by bringing in famous athletes or other celebrities who "believe like we do." This makes "our group" look good to the people who are sensation seekers. There is certainly value in having celebrities give their testimony. We mention this to raise the question concerning the motive of the heart of the people who come as well as their leaders.

We know that many genuine conversions take place through these promotions, and I would not suggest discontinuing them. There are always a few *God-seekers* in the multitude that attends these sensational events. Those God-seekers are represented by the two disciples that left the Baptist to follow Jesus. Big promotions are not wrong in themselves; but we should not be surprised when a large percentage of those who come belong to this second group of self-centered pleasure-seekers.

Mark drew attention to this situation when he told the story of the woman with the issue of blood (Mk. 5). A *crowd* was following Jesus. The woman was in that crowd because she had heard a report (*rhema*) indicating Jesus could heal her. She was willing to press through the crowd and touch his garment to receive that healing. She was singled out from the crowd to receive her healing. But the big following, the *crowd*, was left outside when Jesus went in to raise Jairus' daughter from her deathbed.

The Third Group: Son-Seekers

The third group is much smaller. The initial group of God seekers consisted of the two disciples who hear the simple testimony,

"*Behold the Lamb of God*" (John. 1:36). On that third day the Baptist made a simple declaration of who Jesus IS—not a word about what he offered. The forgiveness of sin and the baptism of the Spirit of the previous day are certainly available to this smaller group as well, but that is not why they began to follow.

Their reason for following was simple. They had heard the testimony, "*Behold the Lamb* of God." They were following because of who he is, not because of some popular expectation of the Christ prevalent in their day. They certainly had some preconceived notions that needed adjusting. However, because they were seeking God and because they were willing to lay their ideas down when Jesus deviated from their expectation, they were true disciples.

On this third day, John set up another sign that reads, "*True disciples follow Jesus because of who he is.*"

Are you among this smaller group or are you still in the crowd? Every self-promoting Pharisee will automatically answer in the affirmative, "Yes. We *are* the smaller group." They always think they are the chosen among the chosen because they measure everything by the standards they have established. And they set those standards based on what they can achieve (or at least appear to achieve) in their own power.

We are all in danger of answering this question too quickly. We may be trying to shield ourselves from the discovery that our balloon is still full of nonsense. We all want to think we are the ones who have arrived. That is why we must all hear the question again and ask ourselves, "What am I trying to find? In all my religious activity, what am I really looking for?"

Being Separated From the Crowd

It is here on this third day that we begin to see true disciples separated from the crowd. Here we observe the real transition. There will always be divisions when Jesus begins to reveal himself and call disciples to follow him. This call will always draw men away from their place in the crowd with its preconceived notions. This does not imply that those in this smaller group have automatically forsaken all their ideas. They still have their notions of how it should happen, but they are separated from the crowd by their answer to this critical question: "*What do you seek?*"

Five Hundred Favored

When we look at the other Gospels, the book of Acts, and II Corinthians, we discover a compelling progression in levels of discipleship as Jesus made himself available to them. The crowd is everywhere. Even unbelievers receive physical blessings from the Lord every day. Out of that crowd Jesus finds five hundred disciples open enough for him to grant a post resurrection appearance (II Cor. 15:6). I call this the *500 club*. Jesus blessed them with this experience because they were still looking for him after his death. They had not remained in the crowd.

One Hundred and Twenty Waited

Out of that five hundred Jesus found one hundred twenty committed enough to remain in the city until the Holy Spirit was poured out (Acts 2:1-4). Many Christians have had awesome experiences of the presence of the Lord, but life gets busy and they are often not around for "*The Event*" that changes history. They may continue to go through life remembering that wonderful experience they had "once upon a time."

They have the promise of eternal life after they die, and they are satisfied with that promise. But they will not become part of the new thing God is doing in their generation. They are satisfied with the "once upon a time" and the "someday over yonder."

Are you seeking the Father's embrace again today?

Seventy Have Ministry

Among the one hundred twenty Jesus found seventy committed enough to be trusted with a mission (Lk. 10:1). Jesus trusted himself and his resources to them. They went out in a ministry of healing and casting out demons.

Personally, I am not satisfied to be among the crowd who receive physical blessings. I want more. I am not satisfied to be among those who have experienced the presence of the resurrected Lord. There is more. I want to be a part of what he is doing in the earth today. I do not want to watch from the bleachers (or the pews). I want to be involved in advancing the Kingdom of God.

Jesus offers ministry to those who want more than an exciting experience. Are you ready to receive Father's embrace, go out from the Father's embrace to embrace others with the embrace with which you are embraced, to comfort others with the comfort with which you have been comforted (II Cor. 1:3-6)? Rise! Let us go deeper into Father's heart.

Twelve Are With Him

Out of the seventy Jesus found twelve to be faithful enough "to be with him" (Mk. 3:14). I am not satisfied to have a ministry. I want to be with him. None of us can be part of the original twelve, but we can be with him and we can have him with us. We can be with him in a more intimate way than merely working for him as a servant. In the final day there will be those who had a mighty ministry of prophesying, casting out demons, and working miracles. Nevertheless, Jesus will say to them, "I never knew you" (Matt. 7:23). He did not deny their ministry; he only said he never had an intimate, knowing relationship with them.

What good is a ministry if he does not know me intimately, if there is no intimacy with him in Father's eternal embrace? Ministry that does not issue from intimacy with the Father has no lasting value for the minister even if the ministry is valid and people receive healing and deliverance. That is what Paul had in mind when he said, "If I give away all I have, and if I deliver my body to be burned, but have not love, I gain nothing" (I Cor. 13).

Three Are Trustworthy

Out of the twelve Jesus found three he could trust enough to invite them to join him in delicate situations. Peter, James, and

John were with him when he raised Jairus' daughter from the dead (Mk. 5:37). Perhaps Jesus did not trust the faith level of the others. These three were also the only ones present when Jesus appeared in the full brilliance of his glory on the Mount of Transfiguration. Jesus does not automatically welcome just anyone to be present with him in this "secret place" of intimacy.

I do not have to understand what all the issues are. I just want to be trustworthy, that is, worthy of his trust in delicate situations. My heart cries for that. I am desperately seeking that intimacy. Like Paul, "I do not consider that I have made it my own. But one thing I do: forgetting what lies behind and straining forward to what lies ahead, I press on toward the goal..." (Phil. 3:13-14).

Two Face the Trial

Of the three Jesus found two courageous enough to stand with him at his trial. Peter and John were willing to follow while others ran into the darkness. When the trials come, many faded into the night to avoid confrontation. We know Peter denied the Lord that night; but he did attend the trial. He faced it in the presence of Jesus—at a distance, yes, but in his presence.

I want to come to the point where I am willing to face confrontations and stand in the presence of Jesus when he is on trial. Redemption is available when I fail in my ability to follow. I know I am redeemed, but I want to be an overcomer (Rev. 12:11).

Are You the One?

Jesus found only one open and vulnerable enough to follow him all the way to the cross—that *other disciple whom Jesus loved.* That was the one who lay at the breast (in the bosom) of Jesus at the Last Supper. He felt and heard his very heartbeat, the heartbeat of the Father.

Why does that disciple have no name? Because *you and I can be that one*!

Father beckons all of us to join the beloved disciple in that place on the breast of Jesus where we can hear his heartbeat. To the degree that we find our place in the Son who is in the bosom of the Father, to that degree we will be willing to go out from that place to share his love with others. I want to be

Nearer my God to thee,

Nearer to thee,

E'en though it be a cross

That raiseth me.

The Church calls John "the Apostle of Love" because he is the "one whom Jesus loves" and because John speaks of love more than all the others. But John is not the only one who is welcome in that place. As I follow Jesus, I enter a Way that leads to being unified with him and with his Father. I can be "one" with him. I want to be among that *"one-ified" many*—the many who are unified in him—who hear Father God's heartbeat of love and become ministers of his love!

Commitment Flows From Desire

The level of our commitment flows out from the level our desire to be with him, to have him with us, and to experience the love of the Father in Jesus. If we reach a place where we permit a mixture in our desire, we will be left behind in one of the groups that never make it all the way. What we seek will determine the distance we are willing to travel on this road *"from the multitude to the one."* Why do I follow him? Is my heart crying for more? What is your answer? What do you hope to gain as you follow him?

I am not satisfied with merely going to heaven when I die. I want my life to make a difference for the Kingdom of God for the next generation. Embracing the cross is the only way to accomplish that.

"Are we there yet?" I will not be satisfied with anything less than the Father's embrace, even if it takes me to the cross. That is what I seek as I stumble on the way. Is your heart crying out for a place there with John in Jesus' bosom? Are you ready for a deeper walk with him?

In Volume two we will look for the meaning of the sign in Jesus' invitation to the two disciples of the Baptist, "Come and see." Where was Jesus going to lead them and what did he want them to see?

www.ingramcontent.com/pod-product-compliance
Lightning Source LLC
Chambersburg PA
CBHW070552050426
42450CB00011B/2823